PULSE

PUMPING LIFE INTO YOUR KIDS MINISTRY

VOLUME 2

KIDZMATTER

EDITED BY **TINA HOUSER**

WITH **BETH** GUCKENBERGER, BRIAN DOLLAR, KENNY CONLEY & MORE

Pulse II: Pumping Life Into Your Kids Ministry

edited by Tina Houser
copyright ©2016 KidzMatter Inc.

Trade paperback ISBN: 978-1-943294-39-8
Ebook ISBN: 978-1-943294-40-4

Pulse is also available on Amazon Kindle, Barnes & Noble, Nook, and Apple iBooks.

For more information, visit KidzMatter.com and follow us at:

 /KidzMatter

 /KidzMatterInc

 /KidzMatter

 /KidzMatter

CONTENTS

CHAPTER I

JUST ADD WATER

GROW YOUR OWN CHILDREN'S PASTOR

BY **TINA HOUSER**

I GET EMAILS AND PHONE CALLS on a regular basis from pastors and lay people who are searching for a children's pastor. Immediately, my heart sinks, because I know what the next question is going to be: "Do you have any names of people we could contact and possibly interview?" Most of the time I have no name to offer them. And, why is that?

There are some unique characteristics that go along with finding a children's pastor.

1. Typically, it's not the greatest paying job. (Just being realistic here.) You don't find many people who like the idea of relocating their family for a job that doesn't pay well.

2. Many children's ministry positions are part-time, especially if a church is adding this staff person for the first time.

3. A high percentage of children's pastors/directors are not the main breadwinners in the family. To relocate would mean that the main breadwinner would have to find a new job in their particular field to support the family. In our present economy, that's not an easy task.

4. Higher education is not preparing ministers for children's ministry. Very, very few Christian colleges have degrees in children's ministry. Many that say they address this ministry do so with one or two classes included under a general ministry degree. I'm glad that we're seeing more schools provide children's ministry education, but they're not doing it at a rate anywhere close to keeping up with the demand.

There are several organizations and companies that provide help in connecting churches with a possible staff person—some specifically for children's ministry—and they do a great job. I always respond to an inquiry by recommending they contact one of these groups as a first option, because the companies gather information and do the preliminary search for a good match. But, the fact is that there are more churches wanting to fill the position than there are qualified people. So, what can a church do in order to find a children's pastor? The answer may be right under your nose. Grow your own!

Our son was a swimmer and often at a swim meet we saw a bumper sticker, t-shirt, or a banner that said, "I'm a swimmer. Just add water." There may already be someone in your congregation who "is a children's pastor", but they need someone to "just add" to them. Is there someone who gets exceptional joy from seeing kids awaken to the truth of God's Word? Is there someone who is open to new ideas, has a knack with people, receives feedback well, is growing spiritually on their own, and gets excited easily? The rest can be learned. You don't necessarily need to look for someone who has a degree in child development, is ordained, and has 10 years of experience. Just add water and grow your own children's pastor!

If you do decide to grow your own, there needs to be a sincere commitment on the part of both the church and the person you are recruiting. The church must understand that this person has a lot to learn and the budget should reflect that. The person the church is investing in must commit time and energy with the understanding this is for the long-term. They will be educated in children's ministry while they are simultaneously pouring into the ministry. It's learn-as-you-go, on-the-job training.

THE CHURCH'S COMMITMENT

Let's look at the church's commitment. In addition to the salary package, there are two main financial investments: conferences and mentoring. There are all kinds of children's ministry conferences available now. Regional and national. Denominational and independent. Curriculum-specific and general. Onsite and online. As part of the grow-your-own process, the church needs to provide funds so this person can attend multiple conferences, especially in the first two years. The first conference they attend should be general in nature with lots of workshop options and an exhibit hall that displays resources from a variety of publishers. The objective is to get a glimpse of all that is available. If the first conference they attend is organized around one specific philosophy of ministry or one particular curriculum, it's easy for a novice to think this is the only way to approach children's ministry. More specific conferences can most certainly come later when they've learned how to determine what is best for their church's ministry. Going to a conference is not a vacation, so the church should not treat it as such. In fact, after attending a conference and being away from family 24/7 for the majority of a week, many churches give an extra day off.

The other financial investment for the church is to provide a mentor for at least one year, but two years would be wiser. A good mentor is someone who has years of experience in children's ministry and has ministered in two or more different settings (small church, church plant, inner city church, mega-church, senior citizen heavy church, different cultures or areas of the country, etc.) so they understand from their background that not all churches operate the same way. A new children's pastor will rely on the mentor to be available to walk through the big picture, as well as work through details that are such a part of this position. It's a great benefit to be able to learn from the mistakes and experiences of others; a veteran can share the scars and the lessons learned, as well as ask probing questions that will help define the recruit's direction.

Everyone needs someone to hold them accountable, and a good mentor will be that kind of partner, in both the professional and private family realms. A young children's pastor—whether that's in age or merely experience—grows quicker when there is someone to help them avoid the potholes.

Because children's ministry has a very definite annual cycle, a two-year mentorship provides the best opportunity for growth. The mentor is there to guide through the rhythm of an entire year, and points out things to the recruit that they might easily overlook ... like, the decision about whether or not to do VBS needs to be made by Christmas and the planning should start in January ... or recruiting is a continual process and needs to stay at the forefront of your thoughts constantly. Then, during the second year the mentor is there to be a sounding board and encourager to push the minister and ministry forward.

THE RECRUIT'S COMMITMENT

If the church has agreed to support the recruit by investing in education through conferences and mentoring, then the recruit needs to be very sure this is the direction they want to pursue. It can't be a this-sounds-like-it-might-be-a-good-thing decision. The recruit must reflect a commitment to excellence. They may not know much about what they're doing at the beginning, but they've got to be committed to reaching for the next step that will make them more equipped. It takes time, energy, and an acute understanding that this is a long-term commitment.

The recruit must be committed to putting in the time and the energy to learn all they can. It's a daily discipline and not putting in the time shows in their growth. When the day's "to do" list is long, and it's tempting to send the mentor an email asking to postpone their time together, they've got to be determined to keep those appointments. When they've set a reading goal, it hasn't been met, and their favorite TV show comes on, they've got to have the will power to click "off" on the remote. It's easy to say, "Sure, I'll put in the time," but when an actual situation is presented, they may have to think twice about what they will choose.

If the church is going to make a huge investment in this one person, both parties must be assured that this is a long-term commitment. The first two years, especially, are going to be full of mistakes, missed deadlines, failure in planning, discipline issues, misplaced words, and mishandled situations with parents ... but it's a time to learn and grow. After two years, the recruit has experience on their side and kids they are attached to. They feel more confident and benefit from seeing kids grow closer to the Lord. They are now doing the investing more than being invested in.

Long-term commitment—staying for years—honors the church that believed in a raw but passionate person enough to say, "We know you can be a great children's pastor. We're going to 'just add water.'"

 Along with enjoying her 7-year-old grandtwins, Tina Houser is the executive editor of *KidzMatter Magazine* and the early childhood ministry faculty for KidMin Academy. She loves all things kidmin and has written 17 books packed full of ideas that actively engage kids with God's Word. Kidzmatter.com, tinahouser.net

CHAPTER 2

OWNERS NOT RENTERS

BY **ADAM DUCKWORTH**

I STARTED OUT IN MINISTRY AS a volunteer. This is why I'm so passionate about the topic of volunteering—because I believe it can change a person's life, and it can change the world into a better place.

The most commonly asked question I have gotten throughout my ministry career is, "How do you get and keep volunteers?" It's one that has an array of answers and I am sure every person out there who has worked with volunteers has an opinion on how to get this done. For today, I'll give you my response to that burning question, and it is a simple answer.

You have to create a volunteer culture of people who are owners and not renters. "Owners not Renters," you ask? What does that mean?

My wife Katelyn and I rent a condo in downtown Fort Lauderdale, FL. We have rented for almost seven years. We moved here in 2008 to help First Baptist Church of Fort Lauderdale implement a strategy that would help impact the next generation. When I came to First there was an outdated kids' ministry philosophy which had kids sitting through the church service the entire time, so we set out to change that. But now we're getting off track ... back to Katelyn.

As I said, Katelyn and I have rented an apartment for seven years now and she refuses to do anything to the apartment aesthetically. She won't paint the walls, change the bathroom fixtures, get new lighting, or update the flooring. Why does she not want to do these things? It isn't because she is opposed to decor changes or even that she doesn't have an opinion on the matter. She refuses to do them because she refuses to invest money in something that isn't hers. She understands that if she invests money in this property there will be no return on her investment—so why would she do anything to it?

Katelyn is a renter.

Owners think differently about their homes. Owners generally invest more money up front so their investment (2008 aside) will pay off when they choose to sell the property. Owners care about the interiors of their homes and want them to be fantastically decorated, ready to receive guests when they arrive. Owners go the extra mile. They care more, do more, execute more ... and generally do all of those things with more passion than a renter does.

We have recently purchased our first home in Fort Lauderdale. It's a pre-construction condominium that will be completed sometime in the fall of 2016 and Katelyn is already thinking about things differently. She has created a Pinterest board full of ideas that she would like to see executed, has pulled paint swatches from the local Home Depot, and has even engaged an interior designer in her process. She is already thinking about things differently. Why? Because she is now an owner.

So why am I harping on the idea of owning and renting property when we're talking about kids' ministry? Here's why. The same principles related to owning and renting a home can be applied to our volunteering and how we approach it.

I've led volunteers my entire adult life. When I was 18 years old I began working part-time at a church and I've never looked back. Working with and leading volunteers has become a passion of mine, so much so that it is oftentimes difficult for me to find the words to describe how much I love it. I hold Hebrews 6:10 (NASB) close to my heart, *"For God is not unjust so as to forget your work and the love which you have shown toward His name, in having ministered and in still ministering to the saints."*

That verse inspired me to help others, to lead volunteers, and to help volunteers know that when you give to a cause bigger than yourself, God will bless it in response.

Throughout my career, I've seen volunteers who have come from all over the spectrum. I've seen a lot of owners ... and a lot of renters. I have seen volunteers who show up for three weeks and never show up again, regardless of the position description they signed saying they would be there for the next 12 months. Those volunteers are renters.

On the other hand, I have seen volunteers who commit to invest in the lives of a few each week and these people have shown up consistently, on time, prepared. They do this because they are passionate about what they are doing—believing that the best way for a kid or teenager to know God is to know someone who knows God. Those volunteers are owners.

So let's go back to our original question: "How do you get and keep volunteers?" The volunteer cultures that I have seen this work the best in have a large population of owners who are volunteering. Those who are currently serving have an extended tenure because they love it. People scratch their heads as to why this group of people would do this for free.

The volunteer cultures with owners have volunteers who ...

- Pick up trash when they see it on the floor.
- Show up early for the pre-service meeting.
- Wear the T-shirt they are encouraged to wear.
- Didn't sign up to serve because they were interested in meeting their future spouse.

The volunteer cultures with owners have volunteers who ... **believe deeply in what they are doing.**

Have you ever been around a group of folks who were just "there"? They showed up because they had to show up. It was almost like they lost a bet. Who would want to be around that? Those folks sure aren't owners. Owners believe deeply in what they are doing. They understand and grasp the vision of what they are volunteering for and go at it full-steam ahead.

Did I mention that owners believe deeply in what they are doing? So deeply that they lose sleep about the kids or teenagers they lead. So deeply that when the thought of coming in to serve on a weekend enters their mind their heart starts to beat a little bit faster. So deeply that they post about how much they love doing what they do on their social media accounts. So deeply that they seek help from local therapy to get through the volunteering. Kidding. Okay, maybe I'm not.

When a volunteer culture consists of volunteers who understand what it means to own what they are doing it becomes a healthy environment where people are united around a common vision, leaders are supported, and a whole lot of quirky fun can be had.

 Adam is the Lead Communicator at Downtown Harbor Church in Fort Lauderdale, FL and is extremely passionate about working with volunteers. If you want to read more about Owners and Renters pick up *Not Normal: 7 Quirks of Incredible Volunteers* by Sue Miller and Adam Duckworth. Twitter and Instagram: @ adam_duckworth; blog: adamduck.com

CHAPTER 3
SELF-ASSESSMENTS
BY BETHANY HAMMER

Sender: Scott

Subject: Don't forget.

Body of email: It's Karen's birthday today.

A FTER THE ABOVE EMAIL, I immediately went out, bought a $10 gift certificate from our church café, wrote Karen a card, and drove it to the post office to be mailed.

Karen had been an employee within the children's ministry department for a little over seven years at the time I received this email. The year prior, it was Karen's 40th birthday, and I did absolutely nothing to acknowledge it. No gift, no card, not even a "Happy Birthday" when I saw her. To be completely honest, it wasn't even on my radar. Not because I don't care and appreciate Karen, but for me personally, I feel appreciated in other ways, such as a college valuing my opinion. I unintentionally overlooked these differences.

This past spring I took my staff through a personality and temperament assessment. What I learned that day about Karen and about myself made a huge difference in how I now maintain a healthy relationship with her. At the conclusion of the training, my children's ministry team gathered and talked about what we learned about one another and how this knowledge could enhance our working relationships. It was there that I learned the impact that a $10 gift certificate and handwritten card meant to Karen specifically.

Apparently the year prior, my lack of acknowledgment of Karen's 40th birthday had made a statement—a statement that I did not value her nor care about her, neither of which were true. So, the following year when she got a "Happy Birthday" card in the mail, she picked up the phone immediately, called her husband at work, and gleefully shared how much it truly meant to her. I sat there in shock. Shocked that I had offended her so badly. Shocked that a card in the mail warranted a phone call to her husband in the middle of his workday. Sad that I had missed out on seven years of acknowledging Karen's birthday. As soon as I got home that day, I got out my calendar on my phone and plugged in all my staffs' birthdays with an annual repeat reminder.

What that particular assessment did that day was a game changer. It opened my eyes to the masterpiece God created in Karen. It taught me that I tend to put the task part of my job before the relational part of my job. This unintentionally leaves people on the side of the road. I am thankful Karen stuck with the team, and since that day, I've made some major changes on how I communicate with Karen.

Many people complete these types of assessments and then do not take action. Excited about findings, information is often recognized and even celebrated. Then managers go on with the minutiae of their workdays. Allow me to offer some suggestions on actions to consider and actions to avoid once you have adminsters self-assessments.

ACTIONS TO CONSIDER

Before you begin, invite the Holy Spirit to guide the process.

If we want to know the way God created us, then we have to be open to what He is saying to us and not just what we think about ourselves. We need to ask the Holy Spirit to reveal to us how we were created. *"But when He, the Spirit of truth, comes, He will guide you into all the truth; for He will not speak on His own initiative, but whatever He hears, He will speak; and He will disclose to you what is to come"* (John 16:13, NASB).

Keep the language alive.

When everyone on the team, volunteer or paid staff, can talk the same language, it's a win. There are a lot of assessments which offer continued learning. Whether it is reading material (books, blogs, or articles) or additional trainings offered, be sure to revisit the conversation often.

Distribute tasks based off of everyone's strengths and weaknesses.

If someone is a people person, assign them to welcome new families. Those who enjoy administration can be given a computer with Excel and they will be happy. Living within our gifts provides outcomes that are more productive and enjoyable for the entire team.

Give the assessment that the church uses to potential hires or volunteers within the ministry.

Thoughtfully consider sharing the assessment with everyone involved in the ministry. Too often when we invite others onto our team, we find people who are just like us. Even in the midst of being a little uncomfortable, it's important to have a wide variety of strengths. Use the results to create a balanced environment for ministry to flourish.

Know who your audience is.

Utilize the results to help you most effectively communicate with others. I know if I'm going to discuss a topic with my senior pastor, I need to give him the details and the outcome, nothing more. Whereas, if I'm going to be working with our associate pastor, I need to come with a set of questions so we can brainstorm the outcome together.

ACTIONS TO AVOID

Don't bash others.

Unfortunately within our humanness, it's easy to look at someone and label them a certain way, especially now that we have this newfound knowledge that the assessment offered. Assessments are meant to be a tool to assist teams in appreciating how one another is made, not to be used as ammunition against them.

Don't limit yourself.

"For You formed my inward parts; You wove me in my mother's womb" (Psalm 139:13, NASB). God doesn't make mistakes ... we do. When findings dictate what people are capable of, we aren't fully allowing the Holy Spirit to shape and mold us. How do we take the information learned about ourselves and still allow the Holy Spirit to shape, mold, and stretch us so we are fully living within the will of God?

Don't make excuses for why things can't get done.

At the end of the day, there is still a job that you were hired to do. Don't take the information and use it as an excuse for why you can't do something.

Don't force outcomes.

A friend of mine went home the day of the assessment and cried because she wanted to have a different outcome. It wasn't until she retook the assessment and realized that she was wrapped up in all she thought she should be that it came out more accurately. Keep in mind these types of tests are self-assessments. We are only capable of learning as much as we are willing to allow the Holy Spirit to teach us.

Don't assume.

Don't assume because an assessment says that you are one way, you will always stay that way. Personalities are constantly forming. Research is showing us more and more that we are still psychologically developing into late adulthood. We serve a God who can and will call us to something beyond what any assessment says we are capable of.

Whether it's Life Keys, Myers Briggs®, Real Colors®, DISC®, or Strengths Finder®, remember that we are living in an earthly world. Celebrate the depth of our Heavenly Creator and what He is capable of when we open ourselves up to the prompting of the Spirit.

Sender: Scott

Subject: Thanks

Body of the email: Karen has always liked her job, but this year I've noticed a difference in her. And as her husband, that's a joy for me to see. I'm so glad she's a part of your team!

ASSESSMENT DESCRIPTIONS

Life Keys

LifeKeys is a 2-day workshop complete with group activities and various self-assessments given. Individuals walk away with value as a human being and a new understanding of who they were meant to be versus the roles they've learned to play.

Myers Briggs®

Myers Briggs focuses on 4 specific areas: world, information, decisions, and structure. Once the assessment is taken, identification will be made in one of 16 distinctive personality types.

Real Colors®

This instrument identifies 4 personality types with the purpose to understand human behavior, uncover motivators specific to each temperament, and improve communication with others.

DiSC®

Dominance, Influencing, Steadiness, and Conscientiousness are the 4 main areas focused on through the DiSC assessment. DiSC helps recognize why people behave in different ways and understand behavior styles so individuals and teams increase engagement, boost morale, minimize conflict, and collaborate more effectively.

Strengths Finder®

Through a web-based assessment, individuals will identify their top strengths within 34 themes. People will use the results to better understand and develop their strengths through increased self-awareness.

Bethany Hammer has served as a children's director for the last 8 years at the church she grew up in. She is a daughter, wife, and mother of 2 children—Joey, age 7, and Lily, age 4.

CHAPTER 4

TEACH ALL THE GLORIOUS DEEDS

SPIRITUAL DEVELOPMENT MARKERS

BY B.A. SNIDER

C an you really teach kids deep biblical truths?"

God tells us clearly in Psalm 78 that we are to *"tell to the coming generation the glorious deeds of the Lord."* Personally, I take that to mean the entire Bible since clearly His glorious deeds start with Genesis 1 and continue through Revelation 22, with an amazing amount of the *"glorious deeds of the Lord"* in between.

In Deuteronomy 6 He tells us when to teach our children—*"when you sit in your house, and when you walk by the way, and when you lie down, and when you rise up."* Again, I take that to mean we're to be teaching our children all the time in whatever we're doing.

So now that we've established that clearly God is telling us to teach our children, how do we do that in today's fast-paced, crazy schedule world?

First, let's start with some characteristics of what our children are like spiritually as they grow and develop. How and what can we teach them from God's Word based on their development?

2- AND 3-YEAR-OLDS

- Cannot think abstractly
- Need simple and concrete examples
- Are curious about everything
- Are physically active
- Have limited small-motor skills
- Twos have a limited 200-word vocabulary
- Threes have a 1,500-word vocabulary

Did you read those last two things on the list? They are learning words so quickly that it is important to put "faith" words into their vocabulary! We begin to teach the vocabulary of faith by presenting Bible stories week after week. Even children this young are able to understand basic Bible truths. Some BIG questions they can answer are:

- Who made you? God.
- What else did God make? God made all things.
- Why did God make you and all things? For His own glory.
- Where is God? God is everywhere.
- Can you see God? No. I cannot see God, but He always sees me.

4- AND 5-YEAR-OLDS

- Attention spans last 5-10 minutes
- Literal thinkers
- Curious
- Active
- Imitative
- Growing in independence
- Talkative
- Developing small muscle control
- Expanding vocabulary
- Formulate ideas through concrete experiences

When teaching 4- and 5-year-olds, it is important to give them concrete experiences. How? Take them on a creation walk to discover all God made. Build the walls of Jericho so they can walk around them and watch them fall. Teach motions when they sing and choose songs that teach great truths like "My God is so big, so strong, and so mighty, there's nothing my God cannot do." Even children this young are able to put their trust in Christ and understand basic Bible truths.

YOUNGER ELEMENTARY CHILDREN

- Think in literal and concrete terms
- Can follow specific instructions
- Have a lot of energy
- Want to please teachers
- Are developing hand-eye coordination
- Think in terms of good and bad
- Enjoy Bible stories and like learning from the Bible
- Understand God's love through personal relationships

- Make conclusions about God in concrete terms
- Do not understand the spiritual nature of God

The relationships younger elementary kids have with their parents and teachers are so important. Remember to take this into consideration if you are rotating teachers every week. I know recruiting is the least favorite job of children's ministry leaders, but it is so important for all ages (not just this one) to have consistency in teachers and to form those lasting relationships. Younger elementary children should be taught stories from the entire Bible as they begin to learn biblical truths. They are not ready developmentally to have a chronological look at the Bible, but they are learning how some stories relate to one another.

MIDDLE ELEMENTARY CHILDREN

Middle elementary children are growing physically, emotionally, socially, and mentally at a rapid rate. How are they growing spiritually?

- Eager for more than just Bible stories
- Starting to relate individual Bible events to the scope of Bible history
- Want to know details and facts in Bible study
- Becoming conscious of self and of sin
- Often begin to feel the need for a more personal relationship with God
- Want to put into action what they have learned

Middle elementary is a great age to integrate Bible stories around themes such as worship, grace, missions, witnessing, trusting God, or servants of God. Because students at this age are developing skills of conceptual thinking, you should be emphasizing discovery of truths from Scripture through comparing, contrasting, and analyzing. At this age, their reading skills are so dramatically improved that it's a great time to encourage a habit of personal devotion time during the week.

OLDER ELEMENTARY CHILDREN

Older elementary students, preteens, or tweens are quickly maturing—physically, emotionally, socially, and mentally.

- Understand the elements of the Christian faith
- Are able to understand the history and chronology of Scripture
- Are developing a value system
- Are finding out what it means to belong to Christ and His church
- Are learning to serve and show love to others on a deeper level
- Need encouragement in daily devotions
- Are learning to put into practice what they know from God's Word

At this age, you do not want to miss the opportunity to lay a firm foundation of the history and chronology of the Bible! It is a wonderful time to help your kids see how God has revealed Himself in His Word through a survey of all the books of the Bible. Remember Psalm 78—The *"glorious deeds of the Lord"* aren't only in Genesis, Exodus, the Psalms, and the Gospels. They are in the laments of the prophets, the failures of the kings, the wisdom of the poetry, and the letters to the churches. You want your kids to see that Jesus is central in all of God's Word, from Genesis to Revelation.

Now that we've laid out some of the spiritual characteristics of our kids, let's dig into more of the teaching. It's important for our children to learn God's Word, not just bits and pieces of stories but the whole story of the Bible. The Bible is one story about the One True God and Creator of the universe who amazingly loves us and wants to have a relationship with us. (Awesome!) In order for us to have that relationship with Him, He sent His Son, Jesus. 1 Corinthians 15:3-4 (NASB) says, *"Christ died for our sins according to the Scriptures, and that He was buried, and that He was raised on the third day according to the Scriptures."* Even as Paul is telling us the Gospel, he is saying that this was what God's Word had told us and that Jesus is the fulfillment of the Scriptures.

Not only do we want our children to know the stories of the New Testament about Jesus' birth, life, death, and resurrection, but we want them to know the stories of the Old Testament that point to Jesus.

- The story of God's promise to Abraham that through him God would bless all the families of the earth (Genesis 12:3) points to that blessing being Jesus.

- The story of God's promise that the blood of the Passover lamb on doorposts would save the Israelites (Exodus 12) points to the Lamb of God, Jesus, whose shed blood would save me.

- The story of God's promise to David that a king from his house would have a throne established forever (1 Chronicles 17) points to our King Jesus.

- The countless Old Testament prophecies, such as Isaiah 9:6, point to the coming of Jesus, the Prince of Peace.

- The fulfillment of all the Old Testament promises point to Jesus Christ as the Son of God in this amazing verse in John 1:14 (NASB): *"And the Word became flesh and dwelt among us, and we saw His glory, glory as of the only begotten from the Father, full of grace and truth."*

These are just a few of the truths that we want our children to grasp as they grow into adulthood. To know and trust Jesus in a personal relationship—the One True God who loves His children with an everlasting love.

It is so exciting to see children begin to understand this legacy of faith they have as promised in the Scriptures. Hebrews 11 is not just a "Hall of Fame" of the Bible. It is the legacy of faith for us and for our children.

Faithfully teach God's Word and wait to see what God does in the lives of your children. You know as well as I do that all of the hard things related to doing children's ministry just disappear when we hear a little child confess his sin and receive Jesus as his Savior. Amen!

So the answer to the starting question, "Can you really teach kids deep biblical truths?" The answer is a resounding "YES."

B.A. was a children's director for 20+ years before coming to Great Commission Publications as marketing director, but her hubby calls her the "Queen of Cut and Paste." She gladly accepts this title as she especially loves teaching the Bible to preschoolers, where cut and paste still comes in handy with real paper and glue, not to mention the computer. Great Commission Publications, gcp.org

CHAPTER 5

A RIPPED HEART

MAKING HEALING DEPOSITS

BY **BETH GUCKENBERGER**

EVER FELT DAUNTED BY THE SHEER NEEDS of the children in whatever room you are standing ? Ever lost patience with a difficult child, meanwhile chiding yourself, knowing he has suffered at home so much? Ever needed to explain to a child that a bully doesn't need to be feared or judged, but prayed for and empathized with?

I first remember hearing this particular analogy when I was in the third grade and some girl was being mean on the bus (to everyone, but I came home and told my mom it was just to me). "I want you to imagine Lori's heart as a piece of paper," she began. After we talked, I felt better. The image of falling paper burned in my mind.

Fifteen plus years later, I recalled that moment when I sat on my mom's counter and found comfort in her wisdom. This time I was surrounded by eighth-graders. They had responded to my call and had traveled to another country where I was living and serving orphans. I had only been there for a month and had invested most of that time in a pair of 11-year-old twin girls. The girls lived in an orphanage with 100 other children who needed a lot more than just my husband and I had to offer. Where do we start? I called everyone I knew—every school, church and family member, begging them to come visit us for a week and serve the children alongside us. I never imagined my first volunteers would be 13 years old.

What can I tell them about this mission? How can I let them know there are hurting children who need our concern, attention, love, prayers? *Really, Jesus, 13-year-olds?*

I waited.

A memory floated to the surface. Lori on the bus, my mother ... yes!

I grabbed a piece of paper and began.

Imagine with me that this piece of paper represents the heart of the orphans you will meet this week. Every one of them has been abandoned or abused; there is no exception. For some, they don't remember the day they were dropped off. They just slowly grew up with the realization that they lived differently than the other children in the village, school, or on TV. For others, however, they do remember the moment they were left, and usually it starts with a lie. They are told they are going to a fair, or a carnival, so they skip off the bus or jump out of the taxi and run towards the other children. It's the only way to physically move a 9-year-old. No kid would get on the bus if he knew he was going to an orphanage. Then, sometime later on that night, it hits them where they are.

If you are the oldest child, you suddenly feel responsible, and wonder from that moment on, how your little brother or sister is eating or sleeping or doing in school. A weight not designed to be carried by a child has been placed on his shoulders. I was talking to a group of girls the other day who were sharing their "first day" memories. Some of them can go back to as early as two years old. They remember what they were wearing that day ... who first picked them up ... what they ate. The impact of that first hit is so strong; they'll never forget it.

"Whenever that initial moment of abuse or abandonment happens, it's like ripping a heart in half" (and I rip the paper). It is a bit dramatic and all eyes are on me.

"Then, after that first rip, more start coming." I continue.

"You are the orphan kid in school." (another rip)

"You aren't invited to someone's birthday party." (another rip)

"You don't feel good, and there isn't anyone who cares." (rip)

"It's your birthday and no one remembers." (rip)

"It's visitation day and no one comes to visit you." (rip)

"It's visitation day and someone comes to visit you and you're confused again when they walk away." (rip)

"You don't play sports in school, or go to school plays, because there isn't anyone to pay the fees, or cheer you on, or pick you up." (rip)

"Sometimes, the subsequential rips happen from other children or workers within the home."

"Other times, it comes from children at school who don't want to sit with you." (rip) "Or it comes on a holiday." (rip)

"Other rips come from punishments they receive that they didn't deserve." (rip)

"Or from words that replay in their minds that were carelessly spoken." (rip)

"Sometimes it comes from other adults who sense they are easy prey and come back to hurt what is already considered damaged goods." (rip)

With each rip the heart gets smaller and smaller and harder and harder, so it's no wonder that when I told that girl, "God loves you and has a wonderful plan for your life," she gave me a look that said, "Great plan. I don't want anything to do with a God who had *this* in mind."

Looking at the confetti of paper now strewn around the room, I look up and confess I wonder most days, what can we do? How can we possibly get started?

My voice thick with emotion now, "I don't have the answer, but I do know it will take more than me to do it."

I look up and find their eyes, "Thanks for just showing up."

When you look at the children gathered in your church, they come with their own kinds of rips. They have been ripped at home or at school. They are ripped on at the bus stop or at recess. They hear messages about themselves, rooted in lies from sources all around. Then they walk into your church (which should look more like a hospital) and you have two choices: favor the healthy or get messy with the sick.

That means picking up the confetti pieces strewn all over the floor of their hearts and start making deposits. Remember their name one week to the next. (deposit) Sit with them, give them a responsibility, praise their work, their memory, their singing voice, their shoes. (deposit, deposit, deposit) Smile, listen, pray. (deposit)

Eventually, what I can testify to is that the child, no matter how broken, will eventually look at you and ask, "Who are you? And why do you care so much?"

In that moment, you have the opportunity to say, "I have been sent to you from God. He loves you, and wants you to know that more than anything else."

Depositing into the hearts of broken children gives the Gospel grit. And that gritty Gospel has been saving lost sheep like you and me for a long time.

 Beth and her husband, Todd, live with their family in Cincinnati, Ohio where they serve as Co-Executive Directors of Back2Back Ministries. Between biological, foster, and adopted children, they have raised 10 children.

CHAPTER 6

MAKE IT COUNT!

KIDS NEED TO HEAR GOD'S STORY

BY LISA DAVIS

SOMETIMES A LIFE IS CHANGED in a moment. Sitting in a stuffy, hot room in the basement of the historic neighborhood church filled with scruffy kids was one such moment. The whole room was quiet. "David" was about to pick up 5 stones to defeat Goliath. I remember the excitement on my aunt's face as she told the story, or rather "lived" the story with us. In my mind's eye I could see the shiny brook. I could hear the yells of Goliath, feel his steamy, hot, stinky breath as he breathed out his raucous challenge. I could sense the fear as David stepped forth in courage toward the giant. This was a holy moment, a moment before a miracle was going to take place. God was stepping down to work through the life of a scrawny boy (and a scrawny blond girl sitting in a Sunday school seat). The whole room could feel the beauty of the moment, the quiet awe of a story told in such a way that all were still, captivated by the power of our big God who could do anything, even defeat giants. I knew full well it was a true story, one that was transcending time and space into my heart, into my mind. In this moment, I also knew that I wanted to do what my aunt was doing—to tell God's stories with joy. It was an encounter with God that would indelibly be written on my heart inspiring me for years to come. It was simply an age-old story told in faith that God used in that moment to speak life into the heart of a little girl.

We must always strive to handle Scripture in such a way that brings eye-opening joy and understanding to the hearts of kids. There are definitely things we can do to improve our presentations to provide optimum enjoyment and attention from the kids with whom we work without the need for un-necessary flash. We don't need to add to the Bible or change it so much that it's hardly recognizable. We can find ways to polish and create compelling presentations that kids will want to hear and will be unforgettable experiences that stick with them for life. We just need to learn to tell it well in ways that kids can understand. For *"All Scripture is inspired by God and profitable for teaching, for reproof, for correction, for training in righteousness ..."* (2 Timothy 3:16, NASB). We often get stuck in monotony with our storytelling. How can we break into something fresh and creative?

PRAY!

Never underestimate the power of prayer. When a story is prayed over and the kids are prayed for, God always shows up. When we rely on His power, not our own, He can do more than we even think or imagine.

PERFORMANCE!

There is nothing boring about the Bible. There are only ho-hum performances. When we work with kids we should strive to never make the stories we share mundane. If we feel it is uninteresting, we will usually deliver a boring performance. If we see it as the most amazing story ever, our teaching will reflect that. How you view the Bible makes a difference.

If the storyteller is unprepared or unrehearsed, the audience will embarrassingly know. If the story is poorly written or not age appropriate, God's Word will not be heard. It should never be simply a show or entertainment, but rather an avenue for proclaiming God's Word.

POLISH!

To be truly effective, it helps to talk through the story, use different techniques and choose the ones that work best. A story becomes really smooth after it has been practiced 3-5 times. Grab your family or friends and practice! Taking time to prepare will help you gain confidence and work out the kinks. At a minimum, read it through three times and know it well. Know where you're going so you don't have to peek at your notes. All the barriers are lifted when there isn't a paper between you and the kids. Especially polish the beginning and end; these are always the most important parts.

POPULAR!

It's hard to compete with the fast paced, ever loved digital world in which kids are growing up. It is tempting to go all digital. The interaction, entertainment, and information that technology provides should definitely be utilized by the storyteller but should only be an enhancement, not a replacement for the spoken story. Video curriculum is not an active form of communication. It is flat, passive, and only one-way communication. John Walsh in *The Art of Storytelling* describes storytelling as a conversation that includes the storyteller, the audience, and God's Word. It's not a one-way dialogue; it has give and take, listening and responding. The ability to sense the Holy Spirit moving enables us to adjust or respond to the audience, to question and clear up confusion, and can only happen in a live setting. Those quiet, captivating, moving moments rarely happen during a video.

PAY ATTENTION TO OTHERS!

A great way to improve one's storytelling is to observe others teaching. Watch someone closely who is exceptional with kids with the intent to learn from them. Also, find a friend who can provide honest feedback on your teaching, noting your strengths and perhaps even some weaknesses.

PICTURE IT!

When you tell a story, you should use enough description that kids can envision it in their minds. You should know your own lesson so well that you can taste it, see it, smell it, and hear it. Incorporate sound, movement, and action. You must see the story in your mind. Hear the thunder, feel the wind, and taste the salty spray. Paint a picture with words. If it is real to you, it will be real to the kids. Jesus created powerful unforgettable moments. If we can help kids experience the story, they will often remember it forever.

PACING!

A story should move at the speed of your wiggliest kid! We live in a fast paced world and must keep our stories moving. The younger the age the more fast-moving and interactive the story should be. You can't turn your back on kindergarten kids. When you do, you're in for trouble. Taking a video of yourself teaching will help you experience your pacing. See what parts of the story they are most interested in. What makes them lose focus? Younger listeners should take an active role in the story—picking up manna, creating a huge thunderstorm, walking to Bethlehem, or putting Moses in the river. Too many words tend to bore kids and they will begin to tune you out, ask to go to the bathroom, or misbehave. Keep it brief and brisk.

PAUSE!

Don't be afraid of using a well-placed pause. This lets the audience breathe. Taking a few moments after describing a scene to let the audience picture it, is important. Pausing right after or right before the climax of the story can build drama and allow for thinking to occur. This gives kids time to visualize the story. "The right word may be effective, but no word was ever as effective as a rightly timed pause." - Mark Twain

PLAYFUL!

A story doesn't simply have to be words. Get the kids involved; let them echo a phrase, sing with you, chant a line, or pull some kids up to act it all out. Take a journey with your kids to different parts of the room. Step out of the narrator role and speak as if you are the characters in the story. Use a ladder or a step stool to change your position on stage. Sit on the floor or speak from within a canoe. Wear a costume and tell the story in first person. Find one really cool prop and bring it onstage to help you tell the story. Mix it up, do the unpredictable, and have fun!

God has wired us to pay attention to stories: big stories, little stories, pretty much any story. There are good stories and bad stories, true stories and deceitful stories. Kids need the truth. The Bible has the most wonderful collection of true stories. Tell them well in ways that lives will be changed. Jesus told stories and often let the story speak for itself. They came to Him in crowds just to hear Him speak. God has given us the greatest collection of stories, the Bible. It tells one continuing story of who God is and what He has done for us. With these stories and the creativity God has gifted us with, we can faithfully proclaim the Good News about who He is and what He has done in ways that kids will understand and hearts will be changed. It is a holy calling. Let's do it well!

PULSE II

 Lisa, Children's Ministry Director of Alderwood Community Church in Lynnwood, WA, delights in telling stories and encouraging others to share the greatest story of all in such a way that kids and adults are captivated by the beauty and love of Jesus. Her family of 6 loves living in the great Northwest and enjoys camping, the ocean, and watching Seahawk games.

CHAPTER 7

THREE CREATIVITY KILLERS

BY **BRIAN DOLLAR**

I REMEMBER THE DAY VIVIDLY. It was one of the most disastrous days in my children's ministry career. I had only been in my position for a while, and I was planning for our Vacation Bible School. We were studying the life of Moses, and I needed something to take it over the top. I needed something "Creative!"

So, I made a classic error. I just simply thought back to the last big event I had attended and figured, "I'll just do THAT!" That last event was called "Hell House." It was a tour through real-life situations and ultimately—through HELL. I thought, "What if I take this idea and apply it to Moses and the Exodus? This will be great!"

The concept of "The Plagues Tour" was to give the kids a real-life experience of what it was like for the Egyptians to go through each of the plagues that God sent upon them. So, I gathered up all the supplies I would need, trained the team on what to do, and the day came for "The Plagues Tour."

We entered the first room. The kids loved it as they watched the illusion of the clear water turning red to symbolize the Nile River turning to blood. "Wow! How did they do that?" I was getting so excited.

We went to the next room that represented the plague of frogs. We had purchased hundreds of tiny plastic frogs from Oriental Trading Company and had a CD of frog sound effects going. The kids loved it. They also loved the next two rooms that had sound effects of flies and gnats to signify those plagues. It was going so well!

But, that's when the tour took a major turn. The kids didn't react so well to the fake cow we had lying in the next room to signify the plague of dead livestock. They were pretty freaked out when we went into the room where the people had been struck with the plague of boils. I thought the leaders had done a great job with the theatrical make-up making those boils look realistic. Apparently, they were a little too realistic.

And, then things went horribly wrong. I had made the mistake of putting several junior high boys in charge of the next plague room—the plague of hail. They sat atop ladders with hundreds of ping pong balls in trash bags. As soon as the doors opened, the boys started pelting the kids with ping pong balls. They were like wanna-be snipers and this was their moment. They smacked one of the girls right in the eye. She was bawling, while the rest of the kids started screaming and running out of the room.

It didn't get much better through the plague of locusts room and the plague of darkness room. Did you know that most young children are actually scared of the dark? Who knew? But, it all came to a disastrous end when we entered the last plague room—the death of the firstborn. I had one of my female leaders in full Egyptian period costume with a baby doll in her lap. The kids walked in as the leader was screaming, "My baby is dead! My baby is dead!" The children refused to go in the room and didn't stop crying for 20 minutes.

Needless to say, the next few days were very busy as I had meetings and phone calls from parents—some curious, some angry—wanting to know what in the world I was thinking when I came up with this idea. Parents are so unreasonable sometimes, aren't they?

Why was this event such a disaster? It's because I made the mistake of falling for one of the three "Creativity Killers."

THREE CREATIVITY KILLERS

DUPLICATION

When you're a young adult (with no children of your own) tasked with the assignment of leading children in their spiritual journey as I was, you feel like a fish out of water. You aren't sure what works and what doesn't work—what will be effective and what will fail miserably.

So, I made a huge mistake that many others in kids' ministry make. I decided to just copy what others were doing. I opted for duplication rather than innovation. This classic mistake of choosing duplication over innovation is not one that is unique to me. This phenomenon happens quite often in the church world. We go to a conference, attend a seminar, watch a YouTube video, or read a blog as someone shares a great concept or strategy. We think, "What an amazing idea!" Then we run straight back to our church and try to duplicate it.

We hear reports of what God is doing in the church down the street or the "hot church" in our denomination, and we try to chase their ideas instead of asking God for His ideas. We do this for a lot of reasons.

Duplication is easier.

When we opt for duplication, we avoid the tough work of seeking God for a vision and strategy to grow our ministry. It's a lot easier to steal someone else's "good idea" than invest time seeking a "God idea."

Duplication is faster.

It doesn't take any time at all to get plenty of cool ideas from church leaders in every kind of ministry. Type the words "children's ministry growth ideas" on your browser, and you'll get over 19 million hits. There are books upon books and conferences upon conferences that provide a ton of great ideas. Don't get me wrong. There's absolutely nothing wrong with books and conferences. I'm a firm believer in attending conferences, networking with other ministries, and reading great books. However, books and conferences can easily become a substitute for seeking God and trusting Him for guidance and creativity.

You see, duplication may be easier and faster, but the problem is ...

Duplication rarely produces eternal results.

Jesus told His followers, *"But seek first His kingdom and His righteousness, and all these things will be added to you"* (Matthew 6:33). What do you "seek first?" Is it conferences, books, message boards, and ministry networks? And then do you go to God only when all those things begin to lose their punch? Instead, you should begin on your knees, seeking His idea that will change your life and ministry.

Perhaps you aren't much of a duplicator. Instead, you suffer from the second Creativity Killer ...

PROCRASTINATION

There's an epidemic of procrastination in kids' ministry. I can't believe how many times I hear people say that they don't start their preparation for Sunday services until Saturday night, and I've heard a lot of reasons why.

FULL-TIME: "My week is so full of other church assign-ments that I don't have time to prepare my lesson until Saturday." (Yet, I get all kinds of Twitter jokes, Facebook up-dates, and countless requests for help in "Clash Of Clans" all week from those same people.)

VOLUNTEER: "I work all week, so I don't have time to pre-pare for kids' church before Saturday night." (Did you watch any TV this week? Then, you just made a decision that your fa-vorite show is more important than the spiritual development of your kids.)

SUPER-SPIRITUAL: "Well, I don't prepare too far ahead of time, because I prefer to be led by the Spirit." (Really? So, the God who knew everything about your children before time began can't inspire you today for what He wants to do in the lives of your children three weeks from now?)

Nothing will kill your ability to be creative like procrastina-tion. Is it any wonder the creative juices don't flow when you are constantly under the stress of last-minute work? Don't let procrastination kill your creativity. YOU CAN DO IT! Work ahead! Prepare. Make time for creative thinking. Get alone and pray. Allow the Spirit to inspire you NOW for what He wants to do down the road!

Perhaps the biggest Creativity Killer of them all is...

DISQUALIFICATION

So many kids' ministry leaders immediately disqualifiy them-selves and say, "I can't do it! I'm just not wired that way!" They allow themselves to believe the 6-word lie that I despise—"I'm just not a creative person."

Many kidmin leaders sell themselves short when it comes to their ability to think creatively. They have decided that God only gifted a few key leaders to be able to create and innovate. They have turned the innovative process into some mysteri-ous, spooky, hokus-pokus type of activity.

Some of you have convinced yourselves that, since I am creative, I must have my own personal "bat cave" type lair where I receive downloads from the angel of creative kids' ministry, and your only hope is to duplicate whatever I'm doing. I have news for you—there is no such cave.

YOU can be creative. How do I know? Because you are child of God! You serve the Creative God with limitless creative ability! Even the most naturally innovative and creative minds are finite. The term finite means "having bounds or limits; not infinite; measurable." But God is infinite. He is "far above all," not limited by any boundaries at all. When you draw only on your own creative resources, it's like drinking from a thimble instead of the Great Lakes.

You were born for creativity! The most innovative people I know? Kids! It's true! When you were a kid, all you needed was a cardboard box and a stick. We were all born creative innovators. Somehow, we allowed society to suppress our creative juices and conform us to the mainstream. We're afraid of getting outside the box. We allow fear to dominate our minds and hearts, and we never become the creative person God wants us to be!

Whether it's Duplication, Procrastination, or Disqualification, don't let any of these three creativity killers keep you from becoming the creative innovator God created you to be. I believe the time is coming when every kidmin leader will have confidence in themselves enough to be able to tap into the creative innovator that lives in each of them. When that happens, we will change the world!

 Brian Dollar has been a kids' pastor since 1992 and is the creator of High Voltage Kids Ministry Resources (highvoltage-kids.com). Brian is the author of several books and has a passion for training kidmin leaders via his blog at briandollar.com. Twitter @briandollar1

CHAPTER 8

NOW YOU SEE ME, NOW YOU DON'T

WHY OUR CHILDREN ARE DISAPPEARING FROM OUR CHURCHES

BY **BRYAN OSBORNE**

M R. OSBORNE, WHERE IS GENESIS AT? Where is Revelation? How do you find verses in the Bible? What does the Bible say about homosexuality? What exactly is sin and why do people go to hell?" These are just a few of the questions that were becoming more and more frequent in my thirteenth year of teaching Bible History in a public high school.

I've had a front row seat to the dramatic decline of basic biblical understanding in progressive groups of teenagers for 13 years. This tremendous reduction of biblical literacy seems to correspond directly to the decline of the Christian worldview, not only in America, but all across the western world.

Rarely, if ever, have we seen such a dynamic and rapid shift in perspective and morality as has taken place in the West these past few decades.

Do you realize that the average weekly church attendance in England has dropped to around 6 percent? Since 1969, many churches in England have shut their doors and been converted into things like clothing stores, museums, theaters, liquor stores, night clubs, and tattoo and piercing studios. This trend is not restricted to England; it's happening all across the United Kingdom and Europe. Not to be outdone, Canada is also apparently shedding its Christianity. A news source documented the steady decline of weekly church attendance over the past 30 years and it predicts it will soon reach the levels of Europe where it's well below 10 percent.

What of the United States? This most "Christianized" nation, how are we fairing? It is probably safe to say that the US has more Christian resources (churches, Bible colleges, books, music options, and TV stations) than any other country has ever had throughout all of history. Yet, for all of our Christian resources, America is seemingly becoming less Christian every day.

UNDERSTANDING THE TIMES

As an educator in the buckle of the Bible belt, I have noticed distinct and rapidly increasing changes in the worldview and morality of my students. Even just 10 years ago students adhering to a biblical worldview about things like homosexuality, evolution, and abortion, would have been in the majority in my classes. Now, I see quite the opposite. Although a large percentage of my students would still claim to be Christians they have adopted the secular worldview on many key issues of today. They're having a type of moral schizophrenia, where out one side of their mouth they claim the Bible to be true and out the other profess beliefs in ideas that are clearly anti-biblical.

In 1 Chronicles 12:32 (NASB) we read, *"... the sons of Issachar, men who understood the times, with knowledge of what Israel should do ..."* and the question I want to put forward is: Do we have understanding of the times? Do Christians understand what is happening in America, all across the western world? Do Christians grasp the response that is needed?

I believe the reason we're seeing the collapse of the Christian worldview today is because the culture has actually invaded the church. What has taken place has been a stealth attack by the enemy on the foundation of Scripture, to undermine the authority of God's Word, in order to undermine the Gospel of Jesus Christ.

THE BIG WALKOUT

George Barna conducted research in 2002 and 2006 that showed approximately two-thirds of the young people in our churches will walk away from the church by the time they reach college age. Think about the implications of this study. For a family with three children, an average of two will walk away by the time they reach college. Grandparents, if you have nine grandchildren, six will walk away, on average.

That is why Answers in Genesis commissioned a major nationwide research project with Britt Beamer and America's Research Group to find out why and when our children are leaving. The astounding results of the research were published in the book *Already Gone*. Beamer's group interviewed 1,000 people in their twenties, male and female, who grew up in conservative churches but have since walked away. From the plethora of data he acquired, let us look at two of the major findings.

First, much to our surprise it was not in college when students were first having major doubts related to the Bible and Christianity, but mostly in middle and high school. In the survey, participants were asked, "If you don't believe all the accounts/stories in the Bible are true/accurate, when did you first have doubts?" The response was that 39.77%

started having doubts in middle school, 43.68% in high school, and only 10.57% said college. What we learned from the research is that most of our kids who walked away left in their hearts and minds long before they ever left physically for college. That's why to Christians it is such a shock that our kids seem to disappear from church. To us, it seems like an instantaneous change, but to them it has been a gradual foundational shift that oftentimes only bares its fruit once the kids reach college age.

Secondly, when asked why they were leaving, one of the major reasons was hypocrisy. When asked what they meant by hypocrisy, the majority responded, "We went to church and were told the Bible was true, trust in Jesus," but then later were told, "... but we don't necessarily believe this part of the Bible," particularly when it came to the book of Genesis and the history found in Genesis 1-11. They heard their Sunday school teachers and pastors say basically, "You can forget about what Genesis says about creation. Believe evolution and millions of years, and reinterpret what Genesis says. That really does not matter. But be sure to trust in Jesus anyway." They see this as hypocrisy and are walking away from the church, and why not! If the Bible can't be trusted when it talks about the beginning, why should we trust what it says about the end? It has no authority.

Psalm 11:3 (NASB) says, *"If the foundations are destroyed, what can the righteous do?"* Today the foundation of God's Word is under attack in the culture and within the church. When we say it's okay to believe what the secular scientists believe about millions of years and evolution and reinterpret vhat God's Word clearly says in Genesis, we undermine the 'story that is foundational to all of the Bible's doctrine, and undermine the authority of God's Word.

we cannot trust the earthly things of the Bible—the clear ~y of the Word of God—then how can we trust the heav- ˜ings (John 3:12, NASB), the message of salvation that is based in that history (1 Corinthians 15:22, NASB) starting in Genesis?

SO WHAT IS THE SOLUTION?

If we're going to truly value our children and youth and strengthen Christian families, we need to be teaching them to stand on the authority of God's Word ... to be able to answer the skeptical questions of this age. We must teach them to defend their faith where the world is attacking today.

Of course, to give them the tools they need, we must first have them ourselves. I Peter 3:15 (NASB) tells us, *"but sanctify Christ as Lord in your hearts, always being ready to make a defense to everyone who asks you to give an account for the hope that is in you, yet with gentleness and reverence."*

In order to be obedient to God's Word, to be ready to give an answer for the faith, we must become intentional about our programming within the church. We need solid biblical curriculum that incorporates strong apologetic teaching based on the foundation of God's Word. We need to show our children and youth how the Bible connects to the real world. We need to show them that the creation account is foundational to biology, the flood is foundational to earth's geology, the tower of Babel is foundational to anthropology, and the fall of man explains death and tragedy.

When we connect the Bible to the tangible world, it becomes alive in the hearts of our youth. It is impossible for me to recount the many times I have seen students have a perception-changing "A-ha" moment when they realize the Bible is real history and can be trusted. For the believer it is major affirmation of their faith; and for the unbeliever it is a challenge to their skepticism and a seed that has been sown. This Anglican hymn writer summarizes the issue well when she says,

"If I profess with the loudest voice and clearest exposition every portion of the truth of God except precisely that little point which the world and the devil are at that moment attacking, I am not confessing Christ, however boldly I may be professing Christ. Wherever the battle rages, there the loyalty of the soldier is proved, and to be steady on all the battlefield besides is mere flight and disgrace if he flinches at that one point." (Elizabeth Rundle Charles)

Don't flinch!

Bryan graduated from Bryan College with a BA in Biblical Studies and received his Master's in Education from Lee University. For 13 years Bryan taught Bible history in a public school and is now a speaker, writer, and curriculum specialist with Answers in Genesis. Answersingenesis.org.

CHAPTER 9

LEARNING THE WORD "NO" FROM BOTH SIDES OF THE FENCE

BY **LUDUSTIA PRISK**

WHEN I FIRST STARTED HELPING IN children's ministry in 1994, the hardest thing for me to do was to say "no." Because I was only part-time, people asked me to volunteer for everything. They assumed that since I did not have a "real job" that I had all the time in the world to dedicate to their project or ministry. My husband was always telling me that I needed to learn to say "no." I was hardly ever home, because I was helping someone somewhere. I had the mentality that if someone needed me to help, then that MUST be where God wants me to be at the moment or they would not have thought to ask me.

I was helping with the Christian Women Job Corp, youth mission trips, and Youth D-Now weekends. I was also helping with events that weren't even church related: babysitting, school events, and concession stands. I had several small paying odd jobs all over town: cleaning, ironing, occasional substituting at school, substituting for the secretary at a dental office. I was tired and burned out and felt as though I was neglecting my family and house.

By the time I felt I was about to step out of my sanity level, I was asked to take over a childcare event that only happened once a year. There was a lot of prep work involved and for very little pay. My husband really did not want me to do it, and after a lot of convincing I finally said "no." The guilt I felt after that was a bit overwhelming. I kept thinking, "But who else will they get to do it? What if no one else steps up? What are they going to do?" No one did step forward and they had to make do in other ways, but guess what? I got over it and so did they. I'm so thrilled that I did not give in. I cannot even imagine how I would have fit that into my schedule!

One specific time when I should not have helped with an event was about 11 or 12 years ago. I was asked to do childcare for a two-day-a-week ongoing event that lasted through the school year. It was a Christian church-based event, not with my church but with a sister church. So, surely that's where God wanted me, right? Well, not too far into the year I realized that was not where I needed to be. The event lasted from 5:15 pm until about 9:30 pm. I found myself dreading going. My own children were there with me, as they were too young to be left alone and my husband's job takes him away from home. There was Wi-Fi in the building but no one would allow my children access to the password to enable them to get their homework completed. (Our school has a 1:1 ratio, laptop to student, and all of their work is done on their computer.) By the time we got home, they were exhausted, but had to stay up another hour or so to get their assignments finished. My children were suffering because of my inability to consider whether an opportunity was from God, or I was just a sucker to agree to help.

Since those two experiences, I found it a little bit easier to say no. It's still not the most pleasant thing for me, but it's getting less stressful to turn someone down. I will pray about it, talk it over with my family and give it a little time before giving my answer. I used to think they had to know right now and I was impulsive with my answer, not giving God or my family a say at all. I still feel a twinge of guilt when I say no. I often have that thought that what if that is what I was supposed to do and I misunderstood God's answer? So I still struggle, even though it is getting easier. I will probably deal with this forever, but I know God will ease the burden I feel.

On the flip side of "no", I have a hard time when I ask someone to help with a children's ministry event and I'm told no. Oftentimes the person will tell me they will pray about it. After a reasonable amount of time, if I've not heard back from them, I assume they are just hoping I found someone else or that I forgot. I will contact them again, and can usually tell if they've forgotten to consider what I have asked or if they have legitimately prayed about it. But when they tell me no, I take it personally. "Why do they not want to help me? Do they not like me, or do they not like children? Do they not agree with what I'm trying to do? Did they really talk to God about this?"

I am still dealing with these issues when someone tells me no. I am still trying to convince myself that when one person says no, it is not the end of the world. I can usually find the right person God intended all along; it just takes longer than I wanted. I am still learning that I need to pray about who to ask before jumping the gun. So many times I just speak my thoughts to the first person I think of without giving God a chance to speak up.

An example of when I've heard "no" and feel it was an impulse answer was when I had asked some retired teachers to help with our after school Awana program. Without a moment's hesitation, they told me, "No, I'm retired. I've done my time." That answer still gets my blood boiling a bit. That's another struggle—those who think they are retired from ministering and will not give it a second thought. They will not pray about it, think about it, talk it over, or ask questions. They just say no.

Hearing someone say no makes me realize how I make others feel when I tell them no. So here we go again, "Do I make them feel like I don't agree with their ministry? Do they think I don't like them? Do they not believe I really considered this and talked it over with God?"

Do you see this vicious cycle I'm in? While I say this is something I have learned in the past year in my ministry, it is something I am still learning and will continue to learn.

I keep reminding myself that Joshua 1:9 (HCSB) says: *"Haven't I commanded you: be strong and courageous? Do not be afraid or discouraged, for the Lord your God is with you wherever you go."* I need to be strong and courageous when I know I need to tell someone no. But I also need not be afraid or discouraged when someone tells me no. God is with me and will help me with these struggles.

Ludustia has been active in First Baptist Church of Floydada, Texas since she was a baby. Her love for children and the fact she is still a child at heart led her to start helping in the nursery department in 1994. Ludustia enjoyed teaching Lil' Blessings Preschool, a ministry of First Baptist Church from 1999-2008, serving as Director those last 2 years. She served as Nursery Coordinator starting in 2003 and expanded her ministry to Director of Children's Ministry in January of 2015.

CHAPTER 10

MESSY, AWKWARD, BROKEN FAMILIES REDEEMED BY GOD

BY CAM POTTS

WHAT MAKES THE PERFECT FAMILY? Is it a certain standard of living or a specific number of kids? Is it making time to eat dinner together or going on vacation as a family? Is it communication or love or forgiveness? Maybe a better question is: Does the perfect family even exist? From the moment Adam and Eve, the first family, took a bite out of the fruit of the one tree God told them not to eat from in the Garden of Eden, sin and brokenness spread to every area of life. There are few areas this is more clearly seen than in the family unit.

Adam and Eve fell into sin in Genesis 3 then in the very next chapter their oldest son, Cain, murdered their youngest son, Abel. The effects of the Fall are the most visible in our family life, because that's where we are our true selves. Sin and brokenness exists in every family because sin and brokenness exists in every person. This reality shows itself on a daily basis through various family conflicts and arguments, but some families experience this reality in more permanent situations, like navigating the transition into a blended family or going through the pain of a divorce. It's these types of situations that have been too often ignored or mistreated by Christians and churches. What does the Bible say about blended families and stepfamilies? Does it even speak to the issue? How should churches approach and walk with families that find themselves in these difficult positions?

For many Christians, knowing where to turn in Scripture to find verses that address hard family situations seems like an impossible task. This is often the case because we tend to view the Bible as having an idealistic (i.e. unrealistic) view of life. The Bible's teaching about how life is to be lived is idealistic only in the sense that it lays out for us how our Creator God intended us to live in every area of life, especially our families. The full spectrum of the experience of family life is presented in Scripture. As I mentioned above, the very first family that ever existed was plagued with issues, and the sin and brokenness didn't stop there. Abraham had a child with his servant, Hagar. It drove a wedge of conflict between he and his wife, Sarah, and one of jealousy between Sarah and Hagar (Genesis 16 and 17). Abraham's grandsons, Jacob and Esau, were strong on rivalry and weak on integrity to the point that Jacob deceived his father, Isaac, in regards to the birthright of the first born (Genesis 25). The drama that existed between Jacob and Leah and Rachel (Genesis 29 and 30) seems more like something you would find in a soap opera rather that in the first book of the Bible. The great King David had a baby with another man's wife, then devised a plan to have that man killed but covered up as a death on the battlefield (2 Samuel 11).

There are numerous examples in the Bible of families that are clearly imperfect. All of the family situations mentioned are messy, wrecked by sin, and painful in one way or another. What is interesting to see, though, is that even in the midst of these broken families, God has a bigger plan that He is unfolding, and it is a plan of redemption. As you look through the genealogy of Jesus in Matthew 1, you will find that many of the people mentioned are from family situations characterized by brokenness and hardship. All of these Old Testament families ultimately led to the birth of the Savior, Jesus Christ, who Himself was born into a family situation that sparked suspicion and gossip among those around them (Matthew 1:18-25). Christians who come from broken homes and blended families are by no means second-class Christians. All Christians are part of God's grand story of redemption, a story that is made up of individuals and families who are being redeemed by God.

While it's easy for us to jump to the practical perspective on things because we are dealing with the nitty-gritty details of each day, it is crucial to keep this overarching story of Scripture in mind. It's the big picture that will provide hope and direction in the midst of daily life. This bigger picture also points us to a larger community that every Christian is a part of—the Church. Every command and truth regarding family life in the Bible is given in the context of community—the people of Israel in the Old Testament and the Church in the New Testament. Family life can be lived in isolation, but God's Word directs our families to point each other towards the Lord and His grace, and that can only happen through intentional involvement in a local community of Christians. As I mentioned above, many Christians and churches carry a stigma toward stepfamilies and blended families that hinders real acceptance and involvement. Therefore, we must carefully think about what steps churches can take to support and encourage these families. Here are a few practical thoughts.

Trust our God. When faced with a hard family situation, it's easy for pastors and ministry leaders to immediately jump in and try to "fix" the problem. Our first step should be to look to our God. We can trust and hope in Him because He is our sovereign God *"from whom every family in heaven and on earth derives its name"* (Ephesians 3:15, NASB). Whatever a family's history or circumstances are, we can trust that God, in His goodness and wisdom, has directed circumstances to where they are now. As pastors and leaders, our focus should be on faithfulness and obedience to God in the present, not trying to rewind to the past or predict the future. Let's commit to pray for these families whether they seek out our counsel or not.

Serve these families. Scripture consistently presents the crucial connection between the church and the home. God has designed life in a way that the family needs the church and the church needs the family. All families face challenges, but those challenges are multiplied in a blended family, and churches must step in to meet needs, big and small. As we seek to meet these different needs, we must be careful not to isolate these families as a separate group in the church. Our efforts to support them and remove the stigma shouldn't have the reverse effect and end up preserving the stigma. The Church itself is a family, united by the Gospel of Jesus Christ that saves us, not by what type of earthly family we come from.

Remember the Gospel. In our local churches we should strive to create a culture where we don't put up hurdles in front of the cross. Some Christians and churches have done this when it comes to family types. We have preached a gospel that says you need to trust Jesus to save you, but you also need to come from a certain kind of family, a family that's not too messy or awkward or broken. In our work to serve all types of families, let's not forget that our Savior came to save all types of people. Perfect families don't exist because perfect people don't exist. Even in the midst of all of our imperfections, we can cling to our perfect Savior who knows our weaknesses and offers mercy and grace to help us in our time of need (Hebrews 4:14-16, NASB).

Cam Potts is husband to Kerry-Lyn and dad to Cooper and Libby. He also serves as Family Pastor to Students at LaGrange Baptist Church in LaGrange, KY. Twitter: cam_potts, Operationparent.org

CHAPTER II

MISSIONARY INTO THE DIGITAL WORLD

REACHING DIGITAL NATIVES

BY **DAVID WAKERLY**

THE MOST POPULAR DESTINATION for children online is YouTube. It used to be that when you asked, "Where are the kids?" you were talking about a physical location. Now, it just might be a digital location in a world called Minecraft.

The kids are in places that just simply weren't places when I was a tiny human. Children don't know life without the Internet. They don't know a time when they didn't have access to the entire history of recorded music. They've never experienced the latest release being booked out at the local video store. And just as an aside, the number one song when teens (who are entering college this year) were born ...

"I Will Always Love You" by Whitney Houston. But this is not an article designed to make you feel old, but instead impress upon you the idea that you and I are immigrants into another culture. We are missionaries trying to reach another world of natives. In fact, the generation born 1995-2009 have been described as "digital natives"—the first global generation shaped by the 21st century connected by devices and engaged in social media. And, there are about 2 billion of them worldwide!

If you are a missionary entering another culture you should know the most important first step ... learn the language. I suggest that, as a leader, you see yourself as an immigrant into another world. Ask questions, seek to empathize and understand a perspective on the world that may be different than yours. So how do you go about being a missionary into the world of children?

BE THERE!

As a missionary into the world of kids, you need to know where they are and be there! As I mentioned earlier, today they are on YouTube. You're not looking to "go viral." You're not looking to make your ministry budget from running ads on your videos. You're looking to simply show up. Your content doesn't need to have perfect artwork with pretty thumbnails for each video, but you need to be there ... on YouTube!

It's highly likely your children know another kid/teenager who is on YouTube. As a 10-year-old watching MacGyver on TV I knew that making a show costs a lot of money and I certainly didn't know anyone making TV shows. It was out of reach ... impossible! Today our children not only know that it's possible that a million people could watch their video in one day, they think they probably could make it.

You cannot afford to not be there. How strange it could seem for a child to see their 10-year-old sister on YouTube but not their 30-year-old kids' pastor? "Does he not know how to upload video?" they silently ask. The creators rule this generation. As the saying goes: "The haters hate and the creators create." If you aren't creating, you're just consuming. In a world where, as a leader, you believe you must influence lives, you need to be a creator!

One of my goals with Hillsong Kids is to avoid creating dualistic lives where the "church world" children know exists separate and apart from the family/school/friend world which they spend most of their time in. I see a generation of children where the kingdom of God is integrated into every area of a life, every moment of the day.

Let me sum this up: Jesus wants kids to come to Him. Be where they are so you can show them the way.

Even YouTube itself knows that kids are huge users of their service. The greatest development recently is the YouTube Kids app (appsto.re/us/U1q23.i) currently launching around the world. This app is designed just for kids; they can discover, learn, and be entertained by videos that are kid approved and family friendly. Parents can now have more control of the YouTube Kids' experience by adjusting the settings such as, turning off "search", reducing the chance that children will find content that they don't want them to watch, or even set a built-in timer to let kids know when it's time to stop watching.

SO HOW DO I DO IT?

Google it. Someone already made an instructional video about it.

But here are a few tips that will set you in the right direction. There are many misconceptions about the equipment you need to make great video. My recommendation is that your phone is enough for video. The cameras in modern smartphones are phenomenal! If you're going to invest in anything, buy audio recording equipment. People will forgive bad video to a certain extent, but bad audio is the number one video creation sin. Your one purpose is to communicate something and if your audience doesn't understand what you're saying, you're wasting your time.

There are microphones available that will plug in to your phone, or you could buy a portable unit with an external microphone. The budget here is from $100 to $1200 for a professional boom microphone. (A good place to start is a Zoom iQ5 or a IK Multimedia iRig Mic Cast.)

WHAT DO I POST?

Here's your first step: Make a video and tell your families about it.

Upload a video that teaches the memory verse that you're teaching your kids on the weekend. Keep it under a minute, and make sure you are well lit or outside (during the day). Don't even introduce yourself. Save that for the end. Get right to the content, straight to the point. At the end introduce yourself and the ministry name, then say, "See you next time."

Play it on a Sunday for your kids. As they are being picked up, put a sticker on each child that says something like "Hillsong Kids is on YouTube. Watch Dave at: youtube.com/hillsongkids." Tell the kids to bug their parents for their phone on the way home. A massive win is 50% of your kids watching.

Winning on YouTube is all about having regular new content, so where to next? Here are some ideas for content.

- Memory verses
- Play video games
- Jokes they can tell Dad
- Preaching messages
- Teaching theme overviews
- Funny promotions for upcoming events
- A weekly series
- Game, book, or music reviews

There are two forms of videos on YouTube—short form, which are videos 1-3 minutes in length and long form, which are videos 4-7 minutes. So make sure you keep your content short and to the point.

The journey of your own channel is all about building subscribers one by one. Here at Hillsong Kids, we started reasonably late in YouTube history, but now have a couple million views and almost 20,000 subscribers. Our most watched videos include memory verse songs and clips that were a hit at conferences or weekend programs that kids want to watch over and over again.

The sky's the limit with where you can take your YouTube channel. You're now creating content that kids can watch at home, watch with their family, and share with friends. Your ministry now extends beyond Sunday and into the mission field where the kids are!

 David is a kids' pastor and Creative Director of Hillsong Kids and has been part of the team at Hillsong Church in Sydney, Australia for over 15 years. He is passionate about children, the generations, and leadership that makes a difference. t:@davewakerley

CHAPTER 12

5 PROS OF SUPPORTING PARENTS

BY **GREG BAIRD**

ARE YOU A CHILDREN'S PASTOR? A family pastor? Do you lead a typical children's ministry? Do you live and breathe family ministry? NextGen ministry?

Here's what I've learned from 25 years in children's and family ministry: It doesn't matter what your title is or what your ministry is called, supporting parents in your ministry is the key to the success of your ministry. In other words, children's ministry is family ministry and family ministry is children's ministry.

But how do we support parents in our ministries, whether children's or family ministry? Here are four important essentials.

I. BE PRO-PARENT

"Pro-parent? Of course I'm pro-parent!" After all, I'm a children's pastor (or family pastor), right?

But sometimes in our ministries we don't act like we are pro-parent. We don't lead with parents in mind. We don't create our ministries in the best interest of parents. Sometimes we don't even consider the interests of parents.

Let's consider just one area of the ministry: program scheduling. Early in my ministry I would become annoyed with parents who couldn't seem to get their kids to what we offered at church (which included weekend services, midweek services, special events, serving opportunities, classes for baptism, etc.). "How hard can that really be?" I would think to myself.

And then I became a parent. As my kids got in to my own children's ministry, I began to understand the challenge. I realized I was scheduling parents right out of my ministry! I was trying to do too much. I wasn't coordinating with youth ministry. I expected every kid to participate every time the doors were open. In other words, it was all about me and my program, not what might be convenient or beneficial to parents.

Scheduling in our ministries is just one example, but there are many areas to consider when we ask the question, "Are we pro-parent in our ministry?"

2. BE PROTECTIVE

Parents are entrusting you with what is the most precious, valuable, and all consuming thing in their lives. They want to know their kids are physically safe when they leave them with you.

Make sure the systems and processes you have in place are sufficient to keep kids safe. Make sure everyone understands them. Make sure they are being followed.

Also, make safety obvious. Communicate safety when families first engage with your ministry. Post safety-oriented signage—"Your child will not be released at check out without the matching tag given at check in" ... or whatever is relevant to your processes. Remind parents that their child's physical safety is important to you and your team.

But don't stop there. Remember that it is not only physical safety that we're responsible for when it comes to the children in our ministry. We are also responsible for the spiritual safety of our children, as well.

What is your plan for spiritual formation of the children in your ministry? If a child were to enter your ministry as a baby and remain there all the way through until they enter youth ministry, how do you know that the teaching they receive is sufficient? That it's comprehensive? That it's theologically correct? That it's everything they need from church in order to have a solid spiritual and biblical foundation of faith?

And what do you do to ensure that the volunteer teachers in your ministry are teaching truth? How do you monitor them? How do you measure success when it comes to teaching volunteers?

Spiritual safety is just as important as physical safety in ministry, yet often we're more concerned about the structure of the program rather than the content of the teaching.

Be protective of your children, both physically and spiritually.

3. BE PROACTIVE

Most parents understand and affirm that the spiritual formation of their children is primarily their responsibility. Most of them would gladly accept that responsibility.

But many parents, if not most, have little idea about how to intentionally invest in the spiritual growth of their children. Most will not ask for help. Usually, the result of this combination is that parents simply do not invest much in the spiritual lives of their children. At best they leave it to the church to influence their children in the spiritual realm.

But this is not enough. It will never be enough, because God designed parents to be the primary spiritual influence in their child's life. For good or for bad, this is always the case.

We, as ministry leaders, need to take up the challenge to be proactive in pursuing parents and equipping them to actively engage in influencing their children spiritually. We need to offer resources, have conversations, and equip parents to spiritually invest in their children in their everyday lives (where the influence is primarily going to take place).

4. BE PROGRESSIVE

We understand that Mom and Dad are going to have the most spiritual influence on their kids. However, we do have a great responsibility when they are with us at church. We can and do make a difference. For this reason, we have an obligation to make sure we're relevant, engaging, and up to date with our ministry program.

When parents see this, it not only helps them feel better about what is happening when they leave their children with us on Sunday, but they will also be more receptive to what we're trying to help them with during the week. An irrelevant ministry on Sunday morning greatly diminishes the relevancy of our voice in other areas. In other words, if you're still using flannel graph, or if your children's area is drab and boring and uninviting ... or if your communications look like something out of the 70s ... you might want to evaluate the relevance of your ministry.

Supporting parents in your ministry is vital to success in your ministry. Being pro-parent, protective, proactive, and progressive are important, but here's the bottom line: supporting parents in your ministry simply means to be **PROFICIENT** at what you do. That's **PRO** #5. Children's and family ministry is "partnering with parents to guide kids toward a heart for God" proficiently. If this is what we do, then supporting parents becomes a necessary consideration in every aspect of our prayer, our planning, and our program.

 Greg Baird has over 25 years experience in children's and family ministry. He currently serves at David C Cook as the Vice President of Global Resources. Davidccook.com

CHAPTER 13

REACHING YOUR COMMUNITY

BY MEMORY PANAYI

T HE SOUTH AFRICAN CONSTITUTION SECTION 15(2) states that government institutions, like schools, can follow religious practices (like having prayers in the morning) but this must be done fairly and people cannot be forced to attend them. The South African School's act confirms this by saying, "Subject to the Constitution and any applicable provincial law, religious observances may be conducted at a public school under rules issued by the Governing Body if such observances are conducted on an equitable basis and attendance at them by learners and members of staff is free and voluntary."

Accordingly, many South African school's governing bodies allow Christian activities at schools, as long as those children of other religions or beliefs are not forced to participate. As a result, many schools will open their weekly assembly in prayer, a Bible reading, sometimes a small message, and most schools even include the singing of Christian songs. This also happens with most end-of-year honors evenings and major sport events.

Hence, we as the South African church have the wonderful honor and opportunity of entering into a partnership with our local schools.

The vision of the church I serve at Woord en Lewe (Word and Life) is Matthew 5:14 (NIV), *"You are the light of the world. A town built on a hill cannot be hidden"*; therefore, each department at our church is encouraged to get involved in our community.

Consequently, our children's ministry (Powerkidz) has a school ministry and by the grace of God, we minister to six different primary/preschools in the area. Our youth department ministers at the high schools. At this stage we have five different teams of volunteers involved in this ministry. We are planning to go to more schools, as our volunteer base increases, since the demand is huge.

We have the honor of attending one assembly per term. Usually, the school is divided into three separate groups according to ages: Grade 0, Grades 1-3 and Grades 4-7. Hence, we see most schools three times a term. We start off with two energetic songs, and then we move into an object lesson, followed by a Bible story, and ending in prayer. In total, we are usually there for 30 minutes. We strive to make our visits very interactive, high energy and fun, but not compromising the Gospel in any way.

The children cannot wait to see us and our visit is usually one of the highlights of their term—all honor to God. Our volunteers always find it amusing when they are walking in the local shopping centers and you see children in their school uniforms with beautiful smiles, bumping a parent, pointing, and muttering, "Powerkidz." It is very precious. We truly feel blessed to be able to do this as we realize the enormous responsibility we have, considering that we are probably the only time some of these children will hear the Gospel.

We are very deliberate in discussing topical issues, for example, bullying and choosing friends wisely. On one occasion we were discussing honoring your parents. For the Bible story I chose Jesus turning the water into wine. After all, Jesus performed His first miracle because He obeyed His mother. We had a little wedding scene with a bride and groom, with one of the children wearing a veil and so forth. Then it came to the part of Jesus turning the water into wine. I had two polystyrene glasses, the one slipped into the other one. The bottom glass contained red mixing cold drink powder. When I showed the children the empty glasses, they did not see the powder in the bottom glass as the top glass obviously masked it, but the children agreed the glasses were empty. We then prayed that God would turn the water into wine. I poured water into the bottom glass and then poured that glass into the other glass. I am sure you can imagine all the "wows" and "no ways" that filled the air as the children saw the water change into "wine." It was a simple illustration that we know they will remember.

On another occasion we arrived at a school only to discover they had already started their assembly. We were worried that we got the times wrong when one of the staff told us they called a special assembly due to an incident. Every time we arrived at this school, you could feel the tension in the air as the majority of their staff was not Christian and we did not feel very welcome. On the way there that morning I even contemplated maybe not including them for the next year, because I thought we were wasting our time, but God knew better. As we stood listening to the principal speak, we heard that two 12-year-old boys got into a fight on the way to school and when the taxi driver (their mode of transport) stopped the taxi, they got out and picked up stones and starting hitting each other. The end result was that both boys were in the hospital. We were horrified, but our lesson that day was choosing friends wisely. Isn't God faithful?

Our Bible story was the Good Samaritan. When we referred to the robbers attacking the Jew, we included hitting him with stones. We kept trying to touch on the incident. At the end we explained to the children that fighting with friends is not from God, and God wants us to choose friends who are a good influence and not friends who are going to pull us down and get us into trouble. After all, what type of friend attacks you with stones?

As we were leaving, in front of the whole school, the principal (also not a Christian) called us back to tell us how we were God sent and how God really used us that day. He said he was so overcome with shock and anger at what the boys had done that he did not know what to say or do, but God used us to explain to the children. All honor to God! Since then, we have had an open door at the school; in fact, the principal said we can just arrive anytime without an appointment and he will call all the children down for an assembly (not that we would do that). God gave us favor and was able to use us. Needless to say, they are now one of our favorite schools to visit.

On another occasion, we got a frantic and desperate phone call from one of the schools. Tragically, one of their grade one learners had passed away the night before. An outside security gate fell on him and crushed him. They had to tell the news to his class and they wondered if we could join them. My husband (one of our senior pastors) and I rushed over to the school. The teacher told them the heart-breaking news and slowly one by one, they started crying. It was a terribly sad occasion, but we could comfort the children and assure them that since we know he believed in Jesus, they would see him one day again, if Jesus also lived in their hearts. They then drew pictures of him in heaven and got much comfort. It was a privilege to be able to be there in their moment of need.

One of the other school's guidance departments contacted us when they were inundated with welfare and counselling cases and couldn't cope. They now partner with our counselling center to help serve the children of our community.

At our church we have big prayer meetings from time to time. A few weeks prior to the meetings we will drop off prayer boxes at the schools and the children can place all their prayer requests in them. At the prayer meeting we pray over all the requests and hold them up in prayer. The boxes are usually full of requests from children and staff. Through this we were able to trace an incident of abuse and refer it back to the school.

At the end of our school year, our schools have an honors evening. This is an evening where they acknowledge the top academic, sport, and cultural achievers for that year. It is quite a prestigious event and something the children work hard to be invited to. At most schools the staff will wear their full academic attire. Due to our association, our pastoral team and I are usually asked to be the guest speakers. This is an awesome privilege and opportunity as we address the parents too.

It took a while to gain trust and prove we do not have any hidden agendas. Slowly the schools are beginning to trust us and we are able to be a beacon of light in our community. Greatest of all, we have had families who did not go to church join our church as a result of the school ministry. God is great! We realize that with big opportunities comes big responsibility, especially when doing God's work. Accordingly, I ask that you please pray for us, for wisdom, favor, and God's covering ... oh, and for more volunteers.

So, why am I sharing about our school ministry with you? Well, my main reason is to encourage other ministry leaders to think out of the box when it comes to serving your community. In our town there are hundreds of churches, yet we are one of the few who go to schools.

I know that in most countries doors are not open in the schools, but you can find other avenues. What about girls and boys clubs, or just have some of your kids help you hand out water at a marathon. Soon, people will be asking who you are and where you come from. That is your opportunity.

Some of us are just going to sow the seeds, others will water, and others will reap the harvest. But all three steps are needed. So let's never fail in doing good, in sowing and in due season you and your ministry will reap a harvest (Galatians 6:9). ,

Memory Panayi is a child of God, wife, mother, pastor's wife, and the Children's Church Director at her local church— Woord en Lewe (Word and Life Church), Boksburg, South Africa.

CHAPTER 14

MARRIAGE, FAMILY, AND MINISTRY

BY JANE LARSEN

THERE'S A CATCHY OLD SINATRA song that goes some-thing like this: "Love and marriage, love and marriage, go together like a horse and carriage ... You can't have one without the other." Can you hear it in your head? If not, you're likely in your 30s or younger. Sometimes in our home we have changed the lyrics just a bit to: "Ministry and marriage, ministry and marriage, go together like ice cream and asparagus!"

As a ministry person, if you're part of a family—any sort of a family—you likely know all too well the challenges that can co-exist with the balancing act of family life and ministry.

Ministry can be completely invasive and overwhelming—evening meetings, phone calls at all hours, interruptions on your day off. It's people's lives, hearts, and needs. There is an urgency. This matters for eternity, right? Certainly God will provide for our families even if we give more to the ministry. He has called us. Right?

"I have no greater joy than this, to hear of my children walking in the truth" (3 John 1:4, NASB). That verse pretty much sums up the goal of it all. It applies to our own children and to those under our influence in ministry. But those in our home are priority above and before the others. We find clear direction from 1 Timothy 3:5 (NASB), *"But if a man does not know how to manage his own household, how will he take care of the church of God?"* How do we do this? How do we do both?

Through God's Word, we see two very clear core issues: idolatry and identity. Gulp. And let me tell you, I have excelled at both.

IDOLATRY

Ministry is valuable. We know it is, whether the world affirms it or not. We know what we do has Kingdom impact. We feel needed. We see God using us and our gifts for His glory. It gives us purpose and worth. But all too easily, we no longer serve God but we serve the work. Ministry becomes our God. The impact it has on our family is profoundly dangerous. We preach "serve your families" and yet we fail to serve our own, because we're busy serving others. When we seek to be all things to all people, what does that look like to our kids? We put ourselves in the rightful place of God—idolatry. When we allow ourselves to be in that position, our families will resent us. Unknowingly, we sometimes let ourselves, our importance, our worth, our impact, become our own god.

IDENTITY

Sometimes the ministry we do becomes a role. We feel needed and it can even feel like acting—far from genuine. There are oodles of people in ministry who need the role and the title to give them worth and value. It could even be you. Too often, we hide behind our calling and let it be the excuse for being out of balance and for messed up priorities. We let a busy ministry have high value, but that's not what God intended for us to do.

So now what? Ask the Lord to show you what the struggle is. Have you put too much on yourself and let the ministry take the rightful place of God? Is your position too important? Do you find yourself needy of the title, the role, the influence more than being whole in Christ simply because He created you and loves you? Be honest and dig deep. Seek the input of trusted friends and ask if they see either of these in your life. Be ready for the answer and don't hold it against them. A true friend will tell the truth because of their love. Ask your family and not just once but often. I learned a great evaluation tool from Dr. Gary Rosberg from America's Family Coaches. "Let's take our temperature. Are we hot or cold?" He would use this phrase with his young children to evaluate how they felt about the family relationships. Check with your family often; they might be hot today and cold next month. Once you know if either identity or idolatry is an issue, own it, and don't make excuses.

Embrace Regrets. I don't really get it when someone has no regrets. I certainly have a bunch of mistakes I've made that I regret. But I do believe those regrets can serve as great teachers—agents for change. The mistakes you have made likely can't be fixed but they can and will be redeemed. Learn from them and do it differently next time.

Self Care. Oh, this is so hard and so very important. Self care involves time off and time with—time off from ministry and time with the Lord. I finally had the a-ha moment that helped me understand the importance of the Sabbath concept. I now take a day fully off—no striving, no work, and all focus on Him. This has had a profound impact on my life. And then time with Jesus. I have always been in the Word and then not. Back and forth. Good devo time one week, not so good the next week. I finally started asking the Lord to get me up early to have time with Him, to let me crave it so much that I was hungry for it. I cannot imagine doing ministry without first being with Him. I had too many years of doing ministry for Him but not with Him.

Tweak Your Thinking. Only one part of our earthly relationships are eternal—brothers and sisters in Christ. Invest the most, the deepest, the best. It's easy to desire what is good, lovely, honorable, and pure, for your spouse and kids when you look at them as your brothers and sisters in Christ. You change your perspective of them. This is one of the most incredible changes in my life. This simple tweak in my thinking has caused my love for my family to flow more freely. It has caused me to pray more effectively for them. I have minimized worry and anxiety. I love them better and am a better wife and mom because of this.

Adopt a Team Mindset with Your Family. Win-win is the only option. Be on each others' side. Always. Say it out loud, "I am on your team." Pray for each other. Pray with each other. Both are needed and yet they are very different. And serve! Serve your family. Ponder this: I serve my family. I serve my spouse. I serve my church. I serve the families. This is consistent from job to home. Instead of being in charge one place or the other, serve both. You will feel a freedom and increased peace in your home.

Don't Compare. Comparison is a deadly trap. Facebook and other social media options are prime ground for cultivating a tendency to compare you and the ministry you serve with to others. Social media has been linked to increased depression and lack of contentment. God has a picture of what your family and your ministry will look like, and you'll find that in His Word as you spend time together. You are wise not to compare to other ministries or to other families. Be confident and content in the family you are.

Do the Little Things that have Big Impact. You can't do it all, but you need to do a lot. You know what matters most, and you know what is essential for you to function well. If you need to walk every day, make it a priority and treat it as an appointment. If you thrive when you have lots of chat time with your spouse, find a way to make it happen every day. For me, having a tidy house is essential. There are five of us (not counting the yappie Yorkie, Baxter). We have a "Ten-Minute Tidy" routine. I set the timer. We all take an area of the house and for 10 minutes we tidy up. That's 50 minutes of manpower. It's amazing how much we get done! You will make time for what matters most.

Know When to be Done. Not with your family. That is a clear, biblical priority. You may need to be done with the ministry, though. Dr. Gary Rosberg said, "Life is short. Your calling is important ... but they can get another speaker, leader, person in your role. Only one person calls you husband/wife and only your kids can call you Mom/Dad. Win at home first."

•••

Since being invited to write this article, a family member has left their spouse and children in pursuit of something "else," leaving behind precious loved ones who are sad, angry, confused, unsure, worried, and quite simply, shattered. Since being invited to write this, a dear friend has had the shock of her husband having an affair and filing for divorce. Theirs is one of those families where you say, "Not them!" And since the invite for this article, a fellow ministry staff member confessed to an extra-marital affair.

Unexpected. Yes. And no, not really. As the thesaurus says, "unexpected" is abrupt, unannounced, unpredicted, and unforeseen. All three of these heartbreakers are that for sure. After pondering these so-very-fresh crisis situations, there were clues. They were at risk. It's wise to learn from the mistakes of others. There are two obvious consistencies between all three: Busyness and Absence.

It's clear that these homes were busy—too busy. Too much work ... too much pursuit ... too much striving and trying and pursuing and seeking more. When anything takes the rightful place of God in our lives, it becomes an idol. Working endless hours, day after day ... doing more ... being out of balance takes a toll. There are seasons of life when that is okay and even demanded, but those seasons are unique and usually temporary, and in those seasons, God provides in a special way. In these families, at least one person was too busy. Too much. They had clearly made choices that were not what God intended for them.

The other issue was absence from abiding in the presence of the Lord. The Word of God is life. We are to hunger for it like we thirst for water. These three were not spending time with the Lord. They were not getting to know Him better. There was no daily feeding from His Word about life and how to navigate the daily challenges it holds. And in one situation, doing work for the Lord took the place of doing life with the Lord. There is a difference.

As you take a serious look at yourself in light of both the ministry and your family, where does busyness and absence fall? Take care of it now! Minister to your family first as you abide in the presence of the Lord. And, may you experience the joy that comes from knowing that your children are walking in the truth.

 Jane Larsen is the wife to Scott and the mom of three kiddos—Alex, Blake, and Emma Grace. Jane serves on the executive team for The Legacy Coalition, a ministry committed to equipping grandparents to impact future generations to know, love, and serve Christ. She leads the kidmin at their church, wears all sorts of hats at the camp Scott directs, and is a true city girl who has found the sweetest joys in rural Iowa, including a darling cow painting that sits right next to her coffee maker! Twinlakesbiblecamp.com

CHAPTER 15

WHAT OLD JIM WISHES YOUNG JIM HAD KNOWN

BY **JIM WIDEMAN**

A WISE OLD MAN ONCE TOLD ME, "Experience is the best teacher, but it doesn't have to be your experiences that you learn from." Every person I know who is successful has learned from a lifetime of mistakes—theirs as well as the mistakes of others. My mom always told me, "Jim, don't make the same mistake twice. There's enough different ones you can make every time." No truer statement has ever been uttered.

Having done children's ministry in my 20s, 30s, 40s, 50s and now my 60s, I've had a chance to make a lot of different mistakes and choices along the way. Would I do things differently if I could go back and do it again? Sure I would. We all would, because hindsight is always 20/20. Forty years ago I could not have taught you leadership. I hadn't learned it yet. Forty years ago I had very few workers. I had a big vision, but didn't know how to make a plan and lead others. I was a hard worker but not a smart worker. The good news is God blessed me in spite of myself. The dreams that were in my heart were not coming to pass. I was smart enough to get some help and to do things differently rather than keep doing what was not working and expecting a different outcome. I'm so glad that years ago I decided that I would become a lifetime learner. I am still learning, but to do so, I have to just say "no" to the know-it-all spirit. So with this in mind, let's look at 10 things I wish Old Jim could teach Young Jim.

1. Don't be a one-man show. Build a team. When you train, empower, and release others, it makes it possible for you to do what only you should be doing. There really is no success without successors, which is a byproduct of team building. Just like in sports the key to continued success is to build depth at every key position. This doesn't happen by delegation alone but by duplicating yourself and the vision into those you lead. Duplication comes through coaching and hands-on training. Young Jim did it all himself. Old Jim allows the team to develop their skills through coaching and encouraging, as well as by doing. Everyone does better with a coach!

2. Watch how you think. Your thinking controls your actions. It moves you forward or holds you back. I was a lot more opinionated when I was younger than I am now. It took me years before I would and could admit that I don't know what I'm doing. That's why it's always smart to evaluate your thinking and choose to think God's way. I love Philippians 4:8 (NASB), *"Finally, brethren, whatever is true, whatever is honorable, whatever is right, whatever is pure, whatever is lovely, whatever is of good repute, if there is any excellence and if anything worthy of praise, dwell on these things."* I wish I did this all the time, but if you're not evaluating how you think on a regular basis, bad stuff happens. It will always work to your favor to think like Jesus. Think in steps. That's how God leads the righteous.

Think like a parent and those you are serving. Think like a visitor. Old Jim has a lot more check-ups from the neck up. Take every thought captive to be obedient to Christ Jesus.

3. Learn from others! Read! Join a local kidmin network. If one doesn't exist in your area, start one. Find a mentor or a coach. (Have you checked out Infuse or kidmincoach.com?)

Study those who are successful. Don't just study what they do, but learn why they do what they do. I have come to realize effective leadership is a process not a pill. Learn the process and the why behind it. Look for a model that you can tweak to fit your church and ministry. Jim, is it wrong to borrow ideas? I sure hope not or I'd be in trouble. Learn how to copy, but at the same time learn how to make the copy your own. Ask questions, tons of them, to anyone who will let you. Also, never be afraid to try what you're learning—experiment with it.

4. Commit to the long haul. Jim, are you telling us when you were younger you thought about quitting? I sure did ... every Monday for a while. It took me a while to stop looking at what I was seeing and have a vision of the finish line. Here are some biggies I wish I had known.

Don't talk about leaving every time you experience pushback.

Be willing to put your dreams on the back burner to serve someone else's dreams. Every dream I ever had came true by being willing to help others see their dreams come true.

Be secure in your calling. If God called you, and He leads your steps, the things you are experiencing good or bad are not a surprise to Him, so trust Him to lead you.

It's my job to remember leading is all about serving. I've found when I am consumed in better ways to serve kids and families—serve those who help you and serve your pastor—it helps me not be the center of attention.

One of the things I'd love to tell young Jim is to be on the lookout for fear.

Anytime fear is around you're about to head backwards instead of forward. Never give into fear. It will always stop you short of the finish line. The two fears that I had to face the most were fear of failure and fear of losing my job. You might face different fears. The key is to face them head on and replace fear with faith.

Another enemy of finishing strong is trying to do everything overnight. Too much too quick is always trouble. Do things in phases or steps, and learn to live by priorities. Have realistic expectations for yourself, and don't stop until you hear God say it's done.

5. Don't take part in power plays! I don't know why even as adults we sometimes act like kids. Don't try to get your way all the time. There's no "I" in team. Old Jim would tell Young Jim that thinking about the well-being of others will always lead you to being the team player you need to be. Look for every opportunity to esteem the team. I've never enjoyed being around pouters, so I have to examine myself and refuse to pout. I'd also tell Young Jim that there's no place for threats in the workplace. Don't threaten to leave, and don't ever pull out the "God said card" in a meeting. If God said it, that's a discussion stopper. Know when you need to lose a battle to win a war. Anytime I enter a negotiation I have to know what I'm willing to give up to take new ground. I've also found out that sometimes it's better to keep your mouth shut and not defend yourself so it will not appear like you're arguing. Old Jim knows God is your Defender and He gives grace to the humble. When it comes to staying away from power plays, don't make someone else look bad to get your way. Old Jim knows that blessed is the peacemaker. Anytime you have the opportunity to make peace, go for it!

6. Take care of your health! Old Jim is being forced to do this today. Exercise, sleep, and good nutrition are essential to you finishing well. Making time for important things is something that will help you at any age. I wish Young Jim knew that making time for exercise has to be a part of your weekly routine, just like meetings and ministry. I know firsthand that everyone makes time for what they really want to make time for. Old Jim would tell Young Jim to make time for the right things. I realize now I've been guilty of working on the wrong temple. Neglecting one to work on the other was not real smart. They both deserve our best and both need a plan of action.

7. The law of the lid determines the quality of leaders I can draw. I didn't realize in my early years of ministry I was holding myself back for not growing my leadership. Go back to number three and put some action steps in place to improve your leadership level. You will never attract workers sharper than you are.

8. Put your family second only to your relationship to God. Do things that your family will remember forever. If I could go back in time, I wouldn't have spent all my vacation time visiting parents and doing ministry. Guard your days off and make them special for your family. Guard your nights. I think it's important that a family church allows for family time. Listen to your family, and be sensitive to their needs. To do that, you have to listen with your eyes as well as your ears.

9. Represent your leader well. Jesus said if you've seen me you've seen the Father. Could this be said of you? Simple things like: dressing appropriately, not being silly, not building loyalties to yourself, and never talking negatively about those in leadership above you. Be your pastor's biggest fan!

10. Be a lover of God's people. The ministry is all about relationships. People matter! I believe the time we spend to empower and encourage people is never wasted. Old Jim knows people are more valuable than programs, meetings, and study. I'm more thankful for the people God has put into my life than the accomplishments I've seen.

People are important to God and should be important to us.

Jim Wideman has been teaching kids and those who teach them for over four decades in the church, as well as in conferences, books, and by coaching. Jim is an OrangeThinker who happens to believe his family is his greatest sermon. Jimwideman.com

CHAPTER 16

10 WAYS TO ENCOURAGE KIDS TO LIVE OUT THEIR FAITH

BY **KRIS SMOLL**

JOSEPH, DANIEL, TIMOTHY, ESTHER, STEPHEN and so many more stood up courageously for their God in the Bible. When you look at the children in your church who have a personal relationship with Jesus Christ, do you see kids who are truly living out what they've been taught? How do you propel your kids forward towards a life of amazingly courageous faith? Let's explore 10 ways to do that through practical ideas, testimonies from kids, and resources that can assist you in the process.

#1 COACH KIDS TO KNOW AND LOVE THE WORD OF GOD.

Where do you begin when encouraging kids to live out their faith? Step one is to challenge them to know and love the Word of God. God's Word is the fuel to ignite a child's passion to pursue the exciting plan God designed specifically for him before time began. Once this forward movement begins in a child's life, we need to be ready to challenge them to use what is pouring out of their soul. A solid biblical curriculum that provides a game plan for long-term discipleship can help you stay on track.

#2 TRAIN KIDS TO CONFIDENTLY SHARE THEIR PERSONAL TESTIMONY.

After a child hears the Gospel and makes the personal choice to accept it, they need to become confident in sharing their personal testimony. A testimony is clearly sharing with others what God has done in a person's life. It has to be more than just a simple statement of, "I became a Christian at church" or "I asked Jesus into my heart." How would this help anyone understand the incredible experience you had when a holy and righteous God sent His one and only Son to die and then rise again so that you can be saved from your sins? Coaching children to share their testimony begins when you verbally role model your testimony to your students and then teach them key Gospel points to be woven into their personal story of life transformation. Create opportunities for kids to share their testimonies in front of a large group such as occasionally setting aside time during the opening worship portion of the morning for kids to share.

#3 TEACH KIDS TO FEED THEMSELVES.

To live out your faith, you need a constant daily fueling of Truth that will fill you. I love using the Awana program in our children's ministries because it's a wonderful tool, if used purposefully, for parents to teach their children how to study God's Word. The weekly routine of working through the Awana books becomes a habit of reading God's Word, understanding the meaning of specific scripture verses, and then memorizing them. These steps create a great foundation in developing the habit of a personal devotional life where kids can feed themselves the Word of God.

Throughout the week, I grow closer to God by reading my Bible everyday; my goal is to read the Bible cover to cover, and I am currently in Leviticus. I also read a daily devotion (Devotions for the God Girl, by Hayley DiMarco). I attend AWANA every week, and go to class every Sunday. I serve with a special needs child every other Sunday. I try to surround myself with good Christian friends, so they can direct me back to God if I ever lose sight. I have some non-Christian friends at school; I talk to them about AWANA or special events at church to give them the opportunity to learn more about Christ. Some of them come to AWANA and other events. I also listen to Christian music, so that I can hear the word of Christ no matter where I am and what I am doing. - Sophie, 6th Grade

#4 MEDITATE ON GOD'S WORD TOGETHER.

Joshua 1:8 teaches us that we should meditate on God's Word, which means to stop and think about it deeply. The attention span of children is dropping as the pace of this world is speeding up. The world's values of speed and constant information saturation totally clash with the ideas found in the word "meditate" and in the verse that tells us to be still, cease striving, and know that I am God (Psalm 46:10). So when and where can you challenge kids to meditate in a world of craziness? Start off by setting aside 15 seconds in your kids' worship set to be completely still and meditate on God. Give them the opportunity to close their eyes, bow their heads, and just think about God's greatness or a scripture verse you've just read. Then encourage them to do the same thing before bed. You need to coach kids to take this time to focus on verses they memorized or lessons they've just studied to help keep their minds on the one true, powerful, awesome God.

#5 CHALLENGE KIDS TO CRY OUT TO GOD.

Prayer can be taught, but genuinely living out your faith means your kids will naturally respond with heartfelt prayer during times of crisis. In the Bible we often hear the statement, "They cried out to God." Do your kids cry out to God? I believe that someone who can cry out to God in times of trouble is blessed with a deeper relationship with Him. Take time to talk to your students about a time you personally cried out to God. Then challenge them to think of a time, place, and situation they met with God and prayed like David or King Hezekiah. Talking about this and role modeling prayer like this will challenge kids to naturally cry out to God in times of crisis outside the walls of church.

Sometimes God puts you through hard times so you get closer to Him ... you run back to Him. - Derek , age 9

#6 EMPOWER KIDS TO EVALUATE THE DIGITAL WORLD.

If our kids' ear buds could speak, what would they say? What is flowing continuously through the minds of our kids via their digital devices? Philippians 4:8 (NASB) says, *"Finally, brethren, whatever is true, whatever is honorable, whatever is right, whatever is pure, whatever is lovely, whatever is of good repute, if there is any excellence and if anything worthy of praise, dwell on these things."*

Living out their faith means your kids should fill their minds with God-honoring words and ideas. How do you coach kids toward positive choices in a digital world? Learn about the digital access they have, and then use that when giving examples and illustrations in your lessons. Teach them to think about the words or actions expressed in video games, music, or movies through a biblical lens. Is it turning them towards God or away from God? Provide both kids and parents with Christian alternatives that are relevant to this generation. Highlight those options during your weekly announcements, incorporate them into your lessons, or play Christian music during an activity. Allow them to see how God has created talented people who use their God-given gifts to honor Him.

#7 GIVE KIDS OPPORTUNITIES TO EXPERIENCE AUTHENTIC WORSHIP.

Worship is more than a bunch of songs to get the wiggles out of kids. It's a time to teach them to truly focus their minds on God and allow them the opportunity to really worship the One True God. How can we facilitate this? Select songs that kids can easily sing so their minds can naturally focus on their God rather than a million words. Be careful not to overdo hand motions; hand motions are a form of worship, not a dance show. They should lead kids towards worship, rather than following body movements with a fun beat.

Give kids opportunities to be bold and loud for their faith. Encourage your kids to sing loudly and proudly; this idea should carry over into their lives outside the church in how they live out and voice their faith.

To help kids learn the songs and worship at home, inform parents where to find the music so they can continue to worship at home. To explore the area of worship further, I recommend a classic children's ministry book, *Teaching Kids Authentic Worship* by Kathleen Chapman.

#8 TEACH KIDS TO RECOGNIZE MIRACLES OF GOD.

Nothing in the Bible happened by luck or chance or circumstance. Challenging kids to see and acknowledge miracles of all sizes is a huge step in helping them understand the power of their God.

Ask kids, "Have you seen God do a miracle?" Make them stop and think about what God is doing right before their eyes. Also, get excited when you see miracles in the Bible lessons you're teaching. Remind kids that the God of Moses is the same God who walks by our side today.

I have seen God do miracles in my life through hard times. This past year the enemy tried very hard to break apart my family. God had another plan and brought my family back together because we kept our faith in Him. Now our family is even stronger! He not only did that, but then He blessed our family with my mom getting pregnant in her old age after being told many years ago it would not be possible. He can make the impossible possible! I want you to know that God does miracles in our everyday lives, big and small, even though we might not see it. - Raeleigh

#9 EXPRESS GOD@WORK.

I saw God@Work! Coaching kids to personally see God's hand at work is one thing. The second step is to challenge them to boldly and clearly communicate what they've experienced. One way to do this is by creating a God@Work video booth for your kids to share. Allow kids to verbalize how they have seen God working in their life or how He has answered prayer. Edit the video into short clips and use as transitions during your kids' worship time.

#10 CREATE SPIRITUAL CONVERSATIONS.

It's one thing to know truth and another thing to have spiritual conversations. What better way for kids to do this than to have spiritual conversations with their parents? For some, this is an easy conversation, but surprisingly, for many it's something new. To encourage and facilitate this, let one of your next door prizes be a gift card kids can use to take their parents out to lunch and discuss what they learned in class. Or, have a simple competition to motivate kids to have spiritual conversations with their parents. You, the teacher, call a few parents two days after class asking if the kids talked with them about what they learned. If the conversation happened, send a gift card for a child/parent date.

Kris Smoll is a graduate of Moody Bible Institute, the Founder and Executive Director of Discovery Land Global, and Children's Ministry Director at Appleton Alliance Church. She loves seeing kids around the world know and grow in their relationship with Jesus, and that's why she's a CM consultant to churches across the globe. Wife to an awesome husband and mother to 2 incredible boys, she is a Green Bay Packer fan who loves sleeping through the games on Sunday afternoons. To explore a new children's ministry program designed for churches who are eager to invest in a long-term discipleship plan, visit DLGlobal.org.

CHAPTER 17

BE AN ADVOCATE

BY **TAMMY FORSYTHE**

ARE YOU AN ADVOCATE FOR YOUR MINISTRY? Do we need to be advocates for our ministries?

We all believe our specific ministry is important, which is true; they are important. How does it work with many ministries in a church and everyone feeling their ministry is important? Do some ministries seem like they get more attention than others? Are others out of sight out of mind? If we don't hear about ministries are they forgotten? We never want to become that staff member always talking about their ministry, always sharing about what's happening, but maybe we should.

Webster states an advocate is a person who argues for or supports a cause or policy, a person who works for a cause or group. So, yes, we do need to be advocates for our ministries. If we don't do this, who will?

We need to stand up for our cause and be willing to argue, fight, defend, promote, and champion our ministry, become an advocate for our ministry. In a church, we just don't think that we would have to argue, fight, or defend our ministry. Being an advocate isn't always an easy or natural thing to be or do.

Becoming the Director of Children's Ministry I have discovered that it's necessary to become an advocate, not only for my ministry, but for the children in our church as well. Being an advocate is a decision one must make in order to succeed or accomplish your plans or projects with your ministry.

I don't believe churches would say these statements are true: children should be seen and not heard, or out of sight out of mind. Sometimes it appears as long as Sunday School is provided, nothing more is needed for the children. When that is the case, one might think those statements have validity to them. What do children's areas look like? Are they fun and inviting to children? Do we provide opportunities for children to participate in main services? Children's choirs are provided, but how often do they sing during the main worship service? When we plan events do we forget about children being there, or are they an afterthought? Does the congregation even know how many children are in the church? If we don't provide opportunities for the children to be seen or to participate in the main service, then the answer is probably no.

Statistics say nearly 80% of people in our churches today decided to follow Jesus before age 18. Fifty percent of them decided to follow Jesus before age 12. Jesus said, *"Let the little children come to me. Don't stop them, because the kingdom of heaven belongs to people who are like these children"* (Matthew 19:14, ICB). Jesus' words tell us how important children are to Him. He had them in the midst of His ministry. We need to have children in the midst of our churches. Children are essential to the growth of our churches.

I've discovered not everyone looks at children the way children workers do. We look at children and see endless energy, excitement, and loads of possibilities. We see these things as positive. We see an eagerness to learn. Children are like little sponges soaking up everything around them. They accept the simple truth that Jesus loves them, no questions asked. I believe that's why Matthew 18:3 (NIV) says, *"Truly I tell you, unless you change and become like little children, you will never enter the kingdom of heaven."* As adults we tend to make things harder than the simple truth of "Jesus loves me this I know."

Our children need to have opportunities to experience Jesus. Many of our children never experience a worship service until they're in elementary school, sometimes even middle school. It should be no surprise to us then when they become of "age" to attend the main worship services the experience is foreign and sometimes they have no desire to go.

One Sunday morning during chapel with my preschoolers we were talking about what "chapel" was all about. We talked about how it was a time for singing songs to Jesus. Adults call this worship. We hear a Bible story and learn about Jesus during chapel. Adults call this the sermon. We always end chapel with a time to talk with God. Adults call this praying. This conversation was prompted by some inappropriate behavior of a few little ones. As we were ending this time I made reference to the fact that our chapel time was much like what their moms and dads were doing down at Big Church with Pastor Stan. I felt a prompting in my spirit which grieved me. I realized my little ones in chapel had no idea what Mom and Dad were doing and probably didn't even know who Pastor Stan was.

It's not feasible for children to be in the service every week. But we do need to be an advocate for times for children to be able to attend the main worship service and to look for special occasions for them. A great one in our church is Palm Sunday. There was a time when we had to campaign for this. We bring all of the children down to the main service. Each child is given a palm branch. When the chosen song starts the children walk up and down the aisles waving palm branches and singing. (And yes, many times there was great discussion over the song. It needs to be child friendly. Our kids love "Lord, I Lift Your Name on High.) Everyone loves it. No, it isn't the same as a normal worship service but it is exposing them to the adult worship service even if it's for only a few minutes.

We all need to feel wanted and children are no exception. Do our children's wings look like the rest of the church? Is it an area where they have to fit in? Or is it an area that looks fun ... an area where children want to be? Do parents wonder if their children matter to the church?

The décor of your children's wing could very well be an area where you need to become an advocate for your children's ministry. The same color palette throughout the entire building is important to some, keeping everything uniform to a degree. Children don't care about those things. They want and need an area where they feel comfortable. As an advocate you might have to fight for and defend your ideas.

Boards of Trustees and Facility Teams are extremely important to buildings. The job of decision making for the upkeep of a church is huge and usually goes unnoticed unless it's disagreed with. The importance of color, pictures on the walls, or whatever your plan is for decorating your children's wing might come across as unimportant to them. This is not to be a negative comment toward these two groups. The price of accomplishing your goal could also play a role in the decision-making. Are the children in your church worth spending the money?

If you're going to champion this type of project make sure you have a plan to present. You need to help them understand why it is so important not just to you but to the continued growth of the church. If children are vital to church growth we need them to keep coming back. Make sure you're ready to answer questions. Be passionate about the importance of your project. If it's your project, don't let someone else try to share your passion for you. Your passion needs to be seen and heard from you. Sometimes you even need to be the squeaky wheel. You need to keep it on the forefront of things. Your trustees have many decisions to make, so don't let your project get pushed to the back burner.

Be an advocate for children's ministry. Don't let the children of your church be seen as a nuisance. We don't want the children of our churches to be forgotten. They need to be mentored, instructed, and discipled. Be willing to do whatever it takes—champion, fight for, promote, and always pray for your children. Children are important to Jesus.

"Be careful. Don't think these little children are worth nothing. I tell you that they have angels in heaven who are always with my Father in heaven" (Matthew 18:10, ICB).

"'For I know the plans I that I have for you,' declares the Lord, 'plans for welfare and not for calamity to give you a future and a hope'" (Jeremiah 29:11, NASB).

Be the advocate for the children of your church so they can imagine the possibilities of the plans the Lord has for them.

Tammy Forsythe is the Director of Children's Ministry at First Friends Church in Canton, OH. She loves working with children and believes she has the best job in the world! She's married to her awesome husband Tom and they have two wonderful boys—now young men.

CHAPTER 18

LIFE STAGES

WHY UNDERSTANDING EVERY LIFE STAGE IS MORE IMPORTANT THAN YOU THINK

BY KRISTEN IVY

FOR THE PAST TEN YEARS, I've had the opportunity to collaborate with church leaders who work with kids and teenagers. Whether we're at a student camp, or at a conference, or sitting down to dinner, the conversations tend to focus on the same shared challenges. Maybe some of these resonate with you.

Parents just don't get it.

Chances are some of the parents you connect with don't always use the resources you give them. Maybe they don't all show up to the events that you plan. Maybe some of the parents you talk to even struggle to transition their role as their kids move from one age group to the next.

Staff don't get each other.

Let's be honest here. We would never say this out loud in mixed-ministry company, but maybe it seems like preschool leaders don't understand theology. They just sing silly songs, or middle school pastors just play a lot of dumb games, or the high school pastor . . . well, where is the high school pastor? I'm sure you like each other, but if you aren't sure about the value of each ministry, it's hard to get on the same page.

Small group leaders don't know what they don't know.

On the one hand, small group leaders can be your best mode of discipleship. Just think about how Jesus discipled the twelve. But your leaders aren't Jesus, and the disciples weren't third grade boys. How can you help cast vision when those you are trying to reach are a little more energetic, less focused, and occasionally so off-topic?

Weekly environments aren't strategic.

You can't control much in ministry, but you can control your messaging strategy. What is the best curriculum to use? How do you customize and contextualize it? Should you write your own? Are videos helpful? Every leader wants to know how to be theologically responsible with the limited time they have. But most aren't sure how to implement a comprehensive strategy that works from preschool through college.

You fail to engage parents through transitions.

We've all lived through Promotion Sunday. It's hard enough just to recruit a sufficient number of leaders, reassign rooms, communicate the changes, and plan for the chaos. But every year some families just don't make the transition. What can we do to bridge the gap for not only kids and teenagers but for the whole family.

If any of these struggles seem familiar, one thing I know for certain is this: **You Are Not Alone.**

About three years ago we started working on a project to address some of these situations. It started because we think there is a better way to . . .

- keep families through transition.
- make teaching strategic.
- train small group leaders to connect.
- align staff so they respect each other.
- help ministry leaders and parents win with their kids at every life stage.

The goal is to help every child and every teenager develop an authentic faith. We want them to trust Jesus in a way that transforms how they love God, themselves, and others. When we say every child or teenager, we mean from birth through graduation and even into the first years after high school. In each life stage, a person is being shaped in a way that will never happen again.

That's why we started the Phase Project. The word PHASE is the key word. We define a phase as a timeframe in a kid's life when you can leverage distinctive opportunities to influence their future.

Kids are growing at an unbelievable pace. Every year they are changing mentally, physically, relationally, culturally, emotionally, and morally. That's why secular companies spend hundreds of thousands of dollars to research their audience. It's why educators spend four years studying child development before they enter the classroom. It's why there are specialists who focus on children and adolescents in every field of medicine.

When you understand phases, it changes your approach.

This is also true for ministry. If you want to impact a child's lifelong faith, you need to know more than just theology. You need to know child development as well.

When you understand phases, it changes how you value each other as a staff.

Understanding phases reveals, for example, how preschool ministry lays a foundation that is significant and theological. You can know that the presence of consistent leaders in that age group will prove to them that the world can be trusted, and that the church can be trusted, and that ultimately God can be trusted.

Understanding phases helps explain why faith concepts need to be conveyed in concrete terms for elementary age kids who aren't thinking in metaphors.

Understanding phases gives an explanation for why games re-engage the mind of a middle school kid in the throes of adolescent crisis. Or the reason your high school pastor spends time away from your church campus in order to be at the local school. You can know that fun will be the bridge that tears down walls, builds trust, and makes it possible to lead a student to a deeper and more personal faith.

When you understand phases, it changes how you partner with families at critical transitions.

You will see that transitions aren't just about moving kids from a classroom on hall A to a classroom on hall B. Transitions are about a family which is moving into a new phase of life.

Around the age of ten, for example, a child is transitioning from concrete to abstract thinking. Things are fundamentally changing for a parent as they relate to their child. Parents at this stage may feel confused, overwhelmed, or frustrated. When you understand the changes taking place between phases, you begin to view transitions as more than just a time to reorganize groups. You see these transitions as a unique opportunity to lean into parents to help them re-engage with their child in a significant way.

When you understand phases, it changes how you teach from preschool through college.

What happens at every phase is critical. But it's not critical to teach all of the information at every phase along the way. What is most helpful for a preschooler to understand isn't what's most helpful for a middle schooler. There are some things you don't need to teach in children's ministry, because it will have a greater impact once they are in middle school.

You begin to ask yourself this question: Are we causing them to learn what is most relevant and most essential for this life stage? A life stage mindset in ministry means that you will develop a scope and cycle that works not only strategically for a particular age group but also across the age groups.

When you understand phases, it changes how you train leaders who work with different ages.

You have to hand your leaders information in bite-sized pieces so they can have a better picture of their role. This will create a common ground for how leaders relate not only with kids and teenagers but also with parents. And it will help set realistic expectations for the role each adult has to play in the life of a kid or teenager.

When you understand phases, it changes how you equip parents.

Ministry leaders are agreeing more and more that partnering with parents is the most effective strategy when it comes to influencing the faith of the next generation. While partnering with parents has become a common value, it's also been a common struggle to engage parents at the level leaders desire.

One reason parents may not engage with us may be that we have not fully supported them. Parents have a responsibility to influence their child's faith, but they also feel the weight of caring for their child's health, education, emotional development, safety, and relationships.

This may be the most compelling reason we believe that understanding life stages is essential to effective ministry. If you want to be effective at partnering with parents, you need to do more than help them understand your weekly message.

What if partnering with parents really means that you exist to support them more than they exist to support you? At every life stage, you have a new opportunity to help a parent ...

- understand the phase and recognize what is changing.
- leverage the phase through practical strategies.
- celebrate the phase at unique milestones.
- navigate the phase by anticipating potential roadblocks.

We a re only three years into our own formal journey to understand more about the phases of a kid's life, but it has already given us new insight into how we lead families.

The more you understand life stages, the more complete your approach to ministry can be. You are able to connect better as a team, more effectively train volunteers, develop a more comprehensive messaging strategy, and most importantly engage families.

 Kristen Ivy is the executive director of messaging for Orange and the director of the phase project. She has her B.A. in education and M.Div., is married to Matt Ivy and mother of 3 kids. She's also the co-author with Reggie Joiner of *It's Just a Phase, So Don't Miss It* (justaphase.com).

CHAPTER 19

NO MORE IGNORING SECOND PLACE

GRANDPARENTS HAVE POTENTIAL FOR POWERFUL INFLUENCE

BY **LARRY FOWLER**

I WAS DEAD WRONG.

My first staff position in a small church was as a youth/children's pastor. To be transparent, I was afflicted with a young man's ego, and saw myself as the be-all and end-all to discipling the kids in my group. It never occurred to me that the parents might be better positioned to influence them. God did use me, but I was so wrong to not consider the parents. *SO wrong.*

I eventually saw the error of my own ego, and moved into a role of training others, but my approach still put the responsibility for discipling children on workers in the church. I trained them with fervor. And I still didn't really consider the role of parents. *Still wrong.*

Then, I saw with new eyes the commandment of Ephesians 6:4, and like many, many others in the early 2000s, became convicted that I had ignored the truth revealed in that verse: Parents are to be the primary spiritual trainers of their children. My approach was forever changed. *Got that part right.*

At the same time, I became a grandfather, and that changed my perspective. After three little ones, my daughter's marriage failed. They moved in with us, and I became both dad and grandpa. I began to have a new fervor—to influence my grandkids. But I was neither the children's worker in the church nor the parent, and I still never thought beyond those grandchildren to a broader ministry implication. *More perspective change, but still more learning to come.*

I was like my friend Wayne Rice, the co-founder of Youth Specialties and one of youth ministry's most respected voices (children's ministry people know him as Mary Rice Hopkins' brother). Wayne told me recently, "For decades, I taught youth pastors that parents had the most influence; grandparents were second, and youth workers were third. It just occurred to me that in all those years, I talked about the first and the third, but never once talked about the second."

Then another verse—that I had read so many times—became new to me: Deuteronomy 4:9, *"... make them [the things of God] known to your sons and your grandsons."* The "and" riveted my attention. I began to study the "generation-to-generation" passages in the Bible. I became passionate about the truth that I had a two-generation responsibility to influence my family. And my desire to be an intentional Christian grandparent grew.

I observed that my peers—other grandparents—often lacked this vision. I looked for books on the subject and found very few. I tried to find videos and found only two series. I work with lots of large churches, and began asking, "Do you have a grandparenting ministry?" None that I asked said yes. (I later found one.) A new calling began to become clearer.

Now I'm on a mission—to help the church, and the grandparents in it, see the model that is in Scripture: that while parents are primarily responsible for the spiritual training of children, grandparents have a secondary responsibility that is nearly as powerful as that of the parents.

I want to see my peers go from being Christian grandparents to being intentional Christian grandparents. I want to see churches recognize this potential for discipleship and begin to equip it. I want to see resource providers develop studies and materials that will encourage and equip grandparents for their role in discipling children.

Here are three reasons why.

Grandparents are second only to parents in their potential to influence children spiritually. They have way more potential than the average children's worker in the church because they have the child's heart, and they usually have way more time with them.

Grandparents are usually highly motivated to influence their grandchildren for Christ. Sometimes it's because of their own failures, sometimes because of the widening chasm between culture and biblical truth, and sometimes because of the lack of interest in spiritual things by their adult kids. They are often more passionate than parents about the spiritual development of the grandkids. Children's pastors tell me that at least ten percent of the children in their ministry are brought by grandparents—some because they have custody, and some because they simply care more than the parents.

Intentional involvement of grandparents in their grandchildren's spiritual development is congruent with the family patterns that are revealed in Scripture. In other words, it is biblical.

On the other hand ...

The role of grandparents is given little attention in churches. Most church leaders have never thought about such a ministry; they properly have a focus on parenting and minister to senior saints, but overlook the group in between—younger grandparents. There are simply too few resources. For the nearly 30 million Christian grandparents in America, there are very few books, videos, blogs, or seminars that address their potential for influence. We can do better.

What must churches do?

Redefine what they mean by "family ministry." Most churches target the nuclear family, but don't think of the exceptions (i.e., grandparents raising kids) or the extended family including grandparents.

Recognize their mental image of a "grandparent" may be wrong. Too many think "senior saints" when they hear the word, but the average age for becoming a grandparent is 47. The emerging grandparent is who we can and must target.

Recognize the passion of this group. They are called "empty nesters" or named by their age group; how much better to name them after their greatest passion (their grandkids)!

Envision them being intentional. I have not found a more eager audience than grandparents when you start talking about their grandkids and how to help them grow spiritually. They are typically much more receptive than parents.

Equip them for ministry. There are many barriers, like uncooperative adult children or their spouses, broken relationships, and distance. They need to know of tools they can use and resources they can find.

Create a core group of impassioned grandparents and launch something—a seminar, a small group, or a class. Just get it going!

HOW DOES THIS IMPACT CHILDREN'S MINISTRY?

If you want it to do that, I suggest you take a new approach to engaging grandparents. Usually we try to guilt grandparents into staying involved, and we get the answer back, "Well, I did my time."

Try the side door since the front one isn't working so well. Get them passionate about ministering to their own grandchildren, and then ask, "If your grandchild was in another city (of course, many are), wouldn't you want a grandparent there to be an influence on your grandkids? So how about you return the favor by being an influence to the kids we have in our church whose grandparents live in another city?

Then, create a position that better allows them to be who they are. One of our best Awana ministries has created an option for game time that is called Grandpa and Grandma Time, where kids who don't want to play can just go sit and talk one-on-one with a grandparent. The kids love it and so do the grandparents.

There is simply incredible potential for grandparents to influence our youngest generation, and we've overlooked that potential too long. Now is the time to harness the wisdom, the resources, the energy, the savvy, and the passion of millions of Christians in America—grandparents.

It's for this cause that I am part of a group launching a new organization—the Legacy Coalition. It will be a coalition of family resource providers that will begin to equip churches to minister to grandparents, and a coalition of churches that will commit to launching and sustaining ministry that envisions and equips the second most powerful influence in the lives of our children.

Watch for it. Join us. Together, let's tap this incredible resource.

PULSE II

After 40 years in children's ministry, Larry Fowler isn't sleeping well at night because God is stirring his soul with the need to engage 30 million potential children's workers in a new way: getting the Christian grandparents in America to be intentional in influencing their grandchildren! He is now founder and chief catalyst of the Legacy Coalition, a new national ministry devoted to envisioning and equipping grandparents for ministry to their precious grandkids. Learn more about the Legacy Coalition at legacycoalition.com.

CHAPTER 20

THE SECRET SAUCE TO MAKING BIG THINGS HAPPEN

BY CINDY FIALA AND PHILIP BYERS

W E ARE ALL SPECIALISTS IN what we do—called, educated, skilled, passionate and in most cases, paid to get the job done. We understand that people outside of our area of expertise don't fully understand what we do, and this would be true. It's part of our job to lead, cast vision, set goals, and develop in order to bring the goals to reality. This all takes a great leader. There is an interesting Catch-22 that happens, however, as we lead forward in our specific areas. Whether you lead a church, a ministry, lead in the corporate world and even in our homes, there is a drift toward exclusion, separation, and division. This drift creates territorialism and territorialism creates the dreaded *SILOS*.

By their very definition, silos are meant to keep something contained and separate from anything else. And the truth is that every ministry leader has been hired to be the champion of that ministry, but when it gets to the point of territorialism and self-containment, it becomes dangerous for the church and limits everyone's ability to do what God is calling each of us to do—reach our communities for Christ and creating an environment where disciples are making other disciples for generations to come.

The hard truth about silo thinking and territorialism is that it reveals less about our strengths and more about our weaknesses and fears. When we drift into silo thinking we fall in the rut of self-protection, self-promotion and self ... well, self everything. Collaboration and integration are the complete 180 of self; we become focused on the bigger picture, the main mission and vision, and everyone begins to push the rock from the same side, rather than trying to push for every other side limiting any traction at all.

Romans 12:3-6a (NASB) says it well:

"For through the grace given to me I say to everyone among you not to think more highly of himself than he ought to think; but to think so as to have sound judgment, as God has allotted to each a measure of faith. For just as we have many members in one body and all the members do not have the same function, so we, who are many, are one body in Christ, and individually members one of another. Since we have gifts that differ according to the grace given to us, each of us is to exercise them accordingly."

We're just better together!

So what is the answer to territorialism and silos? A few years ago we decided to wrestle this topic to the floor and discovered some truths about collaborating and integrating ministries. In doing so, we have broadened our ability to effectively see our mission as a whole working toward one goal and not many, mini-missions working against each other. As we work together, we benefit from the expertise of other people with different gifts and talents. We gain resources and time that we wouldn't have had if we pushed forward on our own. Here are five ways you can integrate ministries and break-down silos.

5 WAYS TO INTEGRATE MINISTRIES

1. Get the Right People in the Room

As a people who like to drive hard to get the right results, we find ourselves asking the question, "Who are the right people?" The people who have different vantage points within the organization are the right people. We need to make sure each vantage point is represented. It's important that everyone knows the objective of the meeting in advance. If your senior leader(s) is not in the room, be sure that your vision aligns with their vision. I (Philip) have found it can be very frustrating and wasteful to head down a path that does not align with your senior leader's vision. Learn from our mistakes. Make sure your senior leadership is on board and you have the right people in the room.

2. Apply The 80% Rule

One of my own (Philip) personal struggles is control. I often have to really ask myself the question: Do I want to be right or do I want to get it right?

When working in a room with a group of leaders, there are usually a lot of opinions and ideas. A few years ago we were introduced to a groundbreaking principle called the 80% rule (thanks to @willmancini and Auxano). The 80% rule is this: It is better to have 100% of the people agree on 80% then 80% of the people agree on 100%. When working as a team, we have to shift our expectations and do a quick check—Are we all 80%? (We use a simple thumbs-up or thumbs-down from each person.) If yes, decision made. If no, keep talking. Is it all about my idea or the best idea winning out? If I truly want a group of people to integrate, then we all have to check our egos at the door. And remember, it's more important to get it right than to be right.

3. Clearly Define the Win

Henry Cloud in his book *Boundaries for Leaders* says that one of the critical roles of the leader is to ensure that everyone has focused attention. Before the team disburses into action, everyone must have a clearly defined focus. If we call ourselves successful after this initiative, what will we accomplish? Name it! Be specific! We call this the "win." Then organize everything you do around the win. Make decisions that help drive toward the win. Then evaluate your effectiveness around the win that your team previous defined (see #5).

4. Assign Ownership

Coming up with a great idea is good, but coming up with the proper plan to execute the great idea is essential. As leaders, we have to assign ownership to each piece of the plan. This is a critical component because this group of people may not typically work together. If it doesn't get assigned ownership then it's likely it will not happen. Accountability is a key ingredient to the accomplishment of any team-oriented task. For example, at the end of your planning meeting make sure that everyone can clearly state back the win and what their role is in accomplishing the win. As we often say, clarity is king.

5. Conduct a Blameless Autopsy

Andy Stanley says, "We evaluate what we value and we value what we evaluate." We call this the blameless autopsy. This step is often one that is overlooked. With a sense of a job well done, we can be quick to move on to the next project or goal. I think this is a step that great leaders won't let their teams miss. The evaluation is necessary because it is often in the reflection that we learn our greatest lessons.

The second element of your blameless autopsy should be to go back to the "win" that you identified (see #3) and then evaluate it. Did we do what we said we were going to do? What numerical data are we seeing? The event we just did might have had some great stories, but did we achieve what we were trying to accomplish? (i.e. Did more first time families show up because of this event? Track it, go to your database and look up that number.) That is the tough question that we must ask.

The third element would be to ask, "What did we learn?" It is often in the stillness after the storm where we have gained our most useful insight. Use this prayerful reflection as a team to determine your success.

One of our church values is Love Story, "Celebrating God's big story and every new one He writes." Story should be the first element of that evaluation. What are the stories that God is writing through the work you have accomplished as a team? Celebrate what God is doing. Celebrate the way He has allowed you and your team to be apart of His work.

One of our recent success stories centered around a whole church integration. We recently developed six core values that we think will drive our church for the years to come. We asked ourselves, "What would be the best thing we could do that would help every person in our church know and understand our values at a deeper level?" Our one word as a church is "family." We decided that the best way to accomplish this would be to create moments where families could have conversations around these values. We organized a six-week worship series centered on the values. We then created discussion questions for every adult small group in our church to discuss. We had all of family ministry (early childhood, elementary, and students) teach on the values with large group time and small group discussion. The buzz that was created by our integration was unbelievable. We had husbands and wives discussing their Sunday sermon in their small group with friends and then having spiritual conversations at the dinner table with their kids. It was some of the most fruitful six weeks of ministry we have seen. We are convinced that it would not have been nearly as productive without the hard work of integration among all of our teams.

At the end of the day, we are still figuring this out or as we like to say, "We're building the plane in the air." But we did push hard to have these conversations, and because of that we are truly better together. We leave our feelings and any personal agendas at the door in order to be "all in." We bring others into the conversation and partner with other ministries within our church.

When people collaborate, when ministries tear down silos and work together, when churches partner with each other, we become and live in the reality of what Christ called us to do! We will see greater things. We will be filled with awe and see wonders and miracles (Acts 2:43). We will have "glad and sincere hearts" (Acts 2:47).

Cindy is the Family Ministry Pastor at Preston Trail Community Church in Frisco, TX. One of her greatest passions is to see ministries integrate and combine efforts for the sake of helping families be all God created them to be. She and her husband John are parents to three plus two and are stupid in love with five-and-a-half grandlittles. FB: Cindy Fiala

Philip is the Groups Pastor at Preston Trail Community Church. His greatest passions are building teams and helping people find and live out God's calling in their lives. He is married to Kelly, who also serves on staff as part of the Family Ministry team, and have 2 active boys—Brady (3) and Deacon (1). FB: byersp / prestontrail.org.

CHAPTER 21

DIVORCE-INFORMED CHURCHES

BY LINDA RANSON JACOBS

‐‐‐

D IVORCE IN OUR WORLD TODAY is no longer a big issue! Does that shock you that this article about children and divorce would start off by saying divorce is not a big deal any longer? Let me clarify by saying: to society, divorce is no longer a big deal. It is pretty much accepted in every realm of society and unfortunately by many in the church. However, to children, divorce is a huge issue.

To a child, the divorce of their parents can be likened to a tsunami that strikes their lives and leaves destruction and havoc in its wake. Nothing is ever the same again. The break-up of their family unit changes the landscape of their childhood.

Recently, there has been a lot of talk and research about adverse childhood experiences or ACEs. The website, ACEs Too High (acestoohigh.com) is devoted to this concept.

The ACE Study findings suggest that certain experiences are major risk factors for the leading causes of illness and death as well as poor quality of life in the United States. It is critical to understand how some of the worst health and social problems in our nation can arise as a consequence of adverse childhood experiences.

Divorce is one of the major traumas identified by the ACE Study and accepted by the CDC (Center for Disease Control and Prevention) in their research of adverse experiences in childhood. While the divorce rate is actually going down, the co-habitation rate is going up. When a child's parents separate or one of the partners leaves, to the child it is the same as a divorce. It is the death of what the child has known as "the family."

HOW DIVORCE AFFECTS CHILDREN

Divorce affects personal relationships.

1. Relationships with each parent are affected because the parents are no longer one unit caring for and concerned about the child.

2. The divorce can negatively impact relationships with grandparents and other extended family members.

3. Children lose friends at school and neighbors as single parents many times are forced to relocate.

Divorce can affect schoolwork.

1. Many children will have to repeat a grade.

2. Some will drop out of school as teens because they are so far behind their peers in their learning ability.

Divorce affects their health.

1. Many will become ill simply because of the chaotic lives they are forced to lead.

2. Some become ill because of high levels of stress which compromises their immune systems.

Divorce also affects a child's religious beliefs and moral lives.

1. Children of divorce are more likely to pull away from the church as young teens. Most will try to attend church until around age 14 and then they fall away.

2. Many teens and now even tweens turn to various substances to lessen the pain of divorce. We are now finding out that even elementary-age children are experimenting with drugs and alcohol.

3. Many more teens of divorce and family crisis are succeeding in suicidal attempts than teens in the general population. In some of our DC4K (DivorceCare for Kids) groups, even children as young as second grade have been found to be contemplating suicide. Some national research shows 10-year-old children are committing suicide.

HOW DIVORCE AFFECTS THE CHURCH

While the ACE Study findings only mention health and social problems, I believe the church is also being greatly affected by divorce. The most damage is to the children. Because the majority of divorcing couples leave the church once the divorce is granted, children are no longer ...

*   Being taken to church

*   Being exposed to biblical teachings

*   Experiencing exposure to church family

*   Having an opportunity to observe the faith walk of older Christians

*   Finding the love of God or having an opportunity to accept Christ as their personal Savior.

If the parents still attend church, rarely is it the same church. Many times children will not only travel back and forth between two homes but also between two churches. Sometimes these are two different denominations. Children struggle with issues such as:

- Do I stand or kneel to pray at this church?
- Do I raise my hands when we sing or do I stand still when I'm at this church?
- Am I supposed to cross myself or not?
- What do they call that man up front again? Is it pastor, mister, priest or what?
- What does Daddy's church believe again?
- Oh no! I forgot I'm not supposed to wear shorts at this church. Hope none of my friends see me today.

EQUIPPING THE ADULTS AROUND THE CHILDREN

Both the adults who care for these children and the adults who minister to them at church need to understand the many things they can do to help these children survive.

Train your leadership teams about the effects of divorce. Sometimes, just understanding what the child is experiencing helps. Encourage other groups in your community such as childcare and school teachers to attend these sessions also. Remember that many children of divorce live in childcare since their single parent has to work long hours just to support the family.

Develop a team of mentors. Retired people and the boomer population can be trained as mentors who can help children with school projects and homework. They can also provide childcare when a single parent has to work late.

Provide parenting classes for divorcing parents. Give parents the research on what their children are experiencing. Provide helpful parenting tips such as keeping consistent routines, giving their children extra attention, how to set boundaries in their home when parenting alone, and how to manage finances.

Build relationships. These kids need healthy relationship skills modeled for them. They need good solid marriages modeled for them and they need to be included in 2-parent homes as in a mentoring capacity. Some children as teens will continue to attend a house of worship when they have built solid relationships with church family.

Train the children with a "how to" manual. Offer to take the child of divorce aside and walk them through a short class like an adult new members' class. Give them pictures or a notebook explaining how your church handles things like praise and worship (raising hands or not), how you do communion, how people pray, what the adult players in the church are called and, above all, the dress code. Encourage the child to keep the "how to" manual with them when they come to church.

Always remember the child of divorce. If you give out memory verses, give the child of divorce only half the verses since they more than likely only come half the time. When they miss, send them a card or text them a message via their parent's phone. When they have to miss, send them home with next week's lesson so they won't feel left out when they return. Remember, they may not get the note about the VBS, fall festival, or the Christmas party and might not know what they are supposed to bring or do for the event.

WHAT THE CHURCH CAN DO TO EMBRACE THESE FAMILIES

- Single parents need relationships. Relationships are the key in bringing and keeping single parents in the church—relationships with people in the church and with Christ.

- They want to be able to contribute to the church family.

- They need understanding of their situation.

- They need acceptance.
- They need to be validated as worthwhile Christians.
- They need encouragement.
- They need people who will help teach their children biblical truths and model strong Christian marriages.
- They need for the church family to realize that they are parenting alone and that is different from parenting with a spouse.

Rarely is a divorce just the division of community property and an assignment of a visitation schedule. Divorce fractures lives, memories, and families. It leaves cracks in the child's beliefs about marriage and in their basic foundation of religious beliefs.

According to heritage.org, in 1950, for every 100 children born that year, 12 entered a broken family. Four were born out of wedlock and 8 to a divorcing family. By the year 2000 that number had risen five-fold and for every 100 children born 60 entered a broken family—33 children born out of wedlock and 27 children suffering the divorce of the parents.

Patrick Fagan, who gave the report above, stated that essentially in our society in 50 years children went from being part of a "culture of belonging" to being part of a "culture of rejection."

When churches become a divorce-informed church, children will no longer feel like they are part of a culture of rejection. They will feel like they belong.

Linda is semi-retired but she still enjoys being around kids. She enjoys having 3 grandsons living close by and visiting her other grandchildren (who live out of town) periodically. She also has a blast running a DC4K group at her church. Blog.dc4k.org, www.dc4k.org

CHAPTER 22

ARE YOUR KIDS A PART OF GOSPEL-CENTERED COMMUNITY?

BY JEFF HUTCHINGS

"Then the LORD God said, 'It is not good that the man be alone; I will make him a helper suitable for him" (Genesis 2:18).

IN GENESIS GOD DECLARES IT is not good for man to be alone. From the beginning God has called people into community. In *Life Together*, Dietrich Bonhoeffer says, "The goal of all Christian community: they meet one another as bringers of the message of salvation." Most churches don't have a problem connecting kids to a community of kids their own age. That is what most churches do in children and youth ministries. The question is how can churches incorporate kids into the adult community? I often get asked how to successfully integrate children into small groups. And, I respond, "When you find out, please let me know."

It can be very difficult to integrate kids into a small group, but the outcome can really impact how kids experience community in adulthood. As parents we're called to disciple our kids and model for them what Christian maturity looks like. Many parents focus their kids' discipleship primarily on knowledge of the Bible. Unfortunately, this is not a complete picture. We need to build our children and provide a full view of the body of Christ and model what it looks like to be on mission together. Mike and Sally Breen in *Family on Mission* say, "The point is that discipleship and mission never really work unless we are able to create a texture of family on mission. If we are going to make disciples and move out in mission, we need to go from managing boundaries to integrating family and mission into one life, a cohesive framework and fabric that empowers a culture of discipleship and mission, not just occasional events and periodic programs." What does this mean for families who are in small groups?

STRUCTURE

What does it look like to include kids in your small group? This is a difficult question and as I discuss this with other family pastors, there is not a consensus on how to include children in small groups. Some people incorporate kids like any adult who would enter. Others have meals and discuss the Bible while they're eating. Some stagger when men and women meet, allowing one parent to stay at home and only bring the kids in occasionally. Aim to understand the needs of the children in your small group and address the needs accordingly. There isn't a perfect way to structure a group. The main thing is that your children are around a community of believers who are being discipled.

BIBLE STUDY

Time to study the Bible is at the heart of many small groups. Kids need to experience adults interacting with and learning from the Bible. It can be very helpful. We see this happening in

Ephesians 6:1. Paul is addressing the church in Ephesus, but in these verses he is specifically addressing children. *"Children, obey your parents in the Lord, for this is right. Honor your father and mother (this is the first commandment with a promise), so that it may be well with you, and that you may live long on the earth"* Ephesians 6:1-3.

Paul knew this letter would be read in the assembly and children were going to hear it! It is good to have kids hear and see adults discussing scripture. As my kids have participated in our discussion, they say silly things and helpful things. They grow in confidence that they are seen, loved, and heard (and it is also good for the adults to see that kids can even contribute).

GOOD FOR THE BODY

It is good for the entire body to be together. My church, The Journey, could be described as non-traditional in many ways. One example is that we do not have affinity-type classes. We believe growth happens best when you have people of different viewpoints and age ranges to help encourage, rebuke, and ask questions of everyone. One of the benefits of putting people of different backgrounds together is that you don't end up with groups of people who never experience the presence of children. Younger adults in our groups need steady, experienced people to invite them into their homes to see what godly homes look like. Families need younger singles to sometimes babysit and provide an outside perspective. The single and the family become part of one larger Christ-centered family.

MISSION

Kids need to be on mission with the church, because kids are part of the church. God is calling us to care for the world in which He has placed us. The mission of the church is not left to the adults; it should include kids. Discipling our children is more important than efficiency or convenience. My daughter is 9 years old and one day when we were walking our dog, she noticed a significant amount of litter near one street corner and throughout our neighborhood. She looked at me and said, "Dad there's a lot of litter in our neighborhood. I think we should have our community meet up and go through the neighborhood and pick up all the trash." Allowing our kids to be in community with us empowers them to believe and understand how God has called them to serve and need others.

FUN

Have fun with your kids in your community! Teach them that church is more than going to participate in a service. It's a time to connect with your brothers and sisters in Christ and to build relationships with those who you are on mission with. Creating shared experiences for all of the people in your community is important. You have the opportunity to practically show your children that church is a joy, not a burden. How are you cultivating that fun? In the past, my community has hosted kickball games and lip sync tournaments. It's fun to watch my kids have fun and to see the people I'm on mission with encouraging my kids and helping them to have fun.

- What kind of small groups do you want for your church?
- Are you helping your kids experience true community?
- How can you help your children have community as the rule, not the exception?

 Jeff Hutchings is husband to Amber and dad to Andrew, Josie, and Ben. He's the Pastor of Family Ministry at The Journey in St. Louis, MO. His family loves cheering for the St. Louis Cardinals, as well as reading about and creating superheroes. gospelcenteredfamily.com, Twitter: @ jeffhutchings

CHAPTER 23

THE CROWN OR THE CAPE

RAISING LITTLE STORY-BEARERS

BY **LORIE LEE**

FROM A YOUNG AGE, we are drawn into story. We dress up as princesses and superheroes living inside our magical and futuristic worlds. Pipe cleaners make crowns and bath towels capes. As parents, long grown up, we marvel at the creativity of our children. Amused and mystified, we watch them. They didn't learn this from us. Typically, *we* aren't the ones walking around the house or grocery store with magic wands and tights. The creative nature of a child reveals itself through imagination and play—in short—story.

I recently witnessed this with my little boy. He's three, going on Evil Knievel. Yesterday, I glanced into his playroom to see him watching one of my husband's motorcycle movies. I'll set the scene for you.

He's enthralled, standing in front of the screen and mouth hanging open. I can't help myself; I pause to see how long this laser focus might last. I don't have to wait long. In a flash, he hops on his little Strider bike and glides across the floor. Suddenly, he stops, pulls up on the handlebars and shouts, "I'm riding a wheelwee!" I try my best not to laugh out loud and disturb this poignant, action-packed moment for either of us. "What is a wheelwee?" you ask. That would be a "wheelie" for any of you non-bike-enthusiasts.

After another zippy glide around the room, I suppose he decides it's time to imitate what he sees on the screen. To my surprise, instead of tumbling headfirst into the cars and trucks he lined up on the floor, he gingerly gets off his bike, one careful leg at a time, sprawls out on the floor with little limbs sprawled every which way, and yells at the top of his voice, "I wrecked!"

What in the world would compel this little guy to "fall" and "wreck" in the middle of his playroom with no supposed on-lookers? Have you ever asked yourself why your little guy is jumping off the arm of the couch as if he's launching himself out of a plane? Why is your little girl's stuffed animal in the "hospital" wearing a tutu on its head? The simple and compelling truth? Story.

The God-given gift of story in children begs the question: What would it look like if children understood that they are a part of the greatest story ever told—God's story?

BEARING HIS STORY

Young and old, story captures our imaginations and presents us with the opportunity to be a part of something bigger than ourselves. The Bible says in Genesis 1:27, *"God created man in His own image, in the image of God He created him; male and female He created them."* Because each of us is made in the image of the Great Storyteller, we have this longing deep within us to be connected to God's Story.

Children are the embodiment of this deep, intrinsic longing for story. They yearn to belong, explore, adventure, and be part of greatness. They go to epic lengths to be active participants in a story that lands them center-stage—smack in the middle of the action, excitement, and drama. Why? Because even as small children, we are hardwired for story.

God's Story began before the world existed, but can be evidenced through the incredible creation story itself. From nothing, God created something—everything, in fact—and as His creation, we are made in His image. We bear His likeness, and more, we bear His Story. It is imperative to remember that the Story we are all part of as God's creation is the movement of His people (us) towards redemption and reconciliation with Him. That is the Story—His great plan.

And He wrote the Story beautifully, right from birth. Children are precious, not merely because they are miniature humans, but because they were uniquely created by God, in the image of God, on purpose and for a purpose. Ephesians 2:10 emphatically states that *"We are His workmanship, created in Christ Jesus for good works, which God prepared beforehand so that we would walk in them."*

When this great truth is imparted at an early age, children have the opportunity to be Story-bearers of creation, forgiveness, love, and kindness in ways that only a child can. Imagine the impact just one little story could have on others. One pregnant, unmarried, girl named Mary ... one precious baby named Jesus ... who grows up to live and die and live again and change the world forever.

LIVING HIS STORY

So what happens to us? As adults we manage roughly 327 roles and responsibilities at once. We get lazy, and frankly, tired. We get enough real-life "story" throughout our day-to-day. Jammed printers, gossip at work, drippy faucets and diapers, traffic, phone calls to return, empty refrigerators, and piles of bills and laundry. To escape, we watch movies, and occasionally pick up a book when we can keep our eyes open at night.

But when do we really come alive? When was the last time you got utterly lost in what you were doing? Answer: Doing what you love—just like kids. Maybe at age 40 that's exploring on vacation, spending time with a close friend, talking to God, drawing or crafting, tinkering in the garage, maybe even singing in the car.

So adults, I'll ask you a few questions. How often are you doing what you love? What would it look like if you lived more alive in God's Story too ... right in front of your children? Imagine the impact your story could have on others.

Through the maze of our roles and responsibilities as citizens, moms or dads, neighbors, sons or daughters, church members, brothers or sisters, and maybe bread-winners, we must maintain perspective on the big picture of life and pass it on to our children. As we teach our kids that they are part of God's story, we must be crystal clear on what God's Story is so we can communicate it simply and powerfully. Communicate the big picture along with the smaller component of how your child plays a part in God's Story—a story that's still very much in progress.

KEEPING HIS STORY

Let's remember whose story we are living. Do you remember what you had for breakfast yesterday morning? Probably not. We are forgetful people by nature and all of us need reminders in our lives to keep us mindful. Joshua was told in Exodus to create "stones of remembrance" for his people so that they would not forget all of the wonders and works God had done for them. For the children within our care, it would be wise to intentionally build "moments of remembrance" into their lives on a regular basis.

Let's make the effort to create situations that teach and remind our children that they are indeed part of God's larger story in the world. They play an important role just as Joshua did centuries ago. Connect the stories of the Bible to their own stories. Help them see that the genealogy in the Bible is there to help us remember, and that they too are a part of it, just like Dad and Grandma and Aunt So-and-So. Remind them that we are grafted in, adopted sons and daughters of God Himself.

Keeping His story means that we as parents, educators, children's workers, ministers, have a unique opportunity to help steer the children within our reach to come into their role, make a difference, and be a part of God's story of love, forgiveness, and inclusion. And lest we forget ourselves, remember, this applies to us adults too. Think about it. There's a reason Jesus told us to become like children. We, His children—young and old—are His Story-bearers.

We can choose to live and love in action. We can choose to continue to encourage our princess-superhero children to live out their stories. Or, we can stifle their creativity and God's own story unfolding in and through them.

What will you choose today? The crown or the cape?

 Lorie Lee is passionate about raising global kids. She started Be Global in Your Local to provide resources to help families raise children who understand and care about the needs of those around the world. beglobalinyourlocal.com

CHAPTER 24

PARENTING SUPPORT GROUPS

PASTORAL CARE FOR FAMILIES WITH SPECIAL NEEDS

BY **DR. LORNA BRADLEY**

I WISH I KNEW THEN WHAT I know now. As a parent of a young child on the autism spectrum I struggled with emotional and spiritual challenges that come with raising a child with special needs. The judgmental stares, the not-so-helpful tips on parenting, the isolation ... all made coping so much more challenging than it should have been. Like any significant life challenge, raising a child with special needs is made easier through support by others on the same journey. A sense of connection and belonging, the genuine empathy of a shared "me too!" moment, greatly reduces stress and increases resilience.

Faith communities that offer support groups for parents of children with special needs open a vital pathway to pastoral care. Support groups relieve isolation, help individuals process emotions, create an avenue of respite and self-care, and provide a sound theological understanding of God's presence in the midst of special needs. They also improve personal and family resilience. According to a study by Erik Carter and Courtney Taylor of Vanderbilt University, 71% of special needs parents surveyed wanted a support group through their church, yet only 12% of their churches met their need.

Support groups are actually pretty easy to start and sustain. Whereas some special needs ministries may require many volunteers, a support group needs three things: a leader with good people and organizational skills, a place to meet, and a format for sharing emotional and spiritual support. When beginning a new group it is important to include special needs parents in the planning process so that the group meets their particular needs for time, location, and interests. Here are some strategies for starting and sustaining a group.

Empower a discussion leader. This person could be clergy or a layperson. They may have a family member with special needs, but that is not required. Stephen Ministers or care ministry members with gifts of compassion can facilitate discussions. Mainly, the leader needs to be skilled at facilitating discussions and good with follow-up and details, such as sharing prayer requests, keeping the roster current, emailing reminders, following up if someone stops attending, and so forth. The leader is the glue that holds the group together.

Choose a location. Groups can meet at church, in a home, coffee shop, or local community center. Ideally, the meeting should be in a space where people feel comfortable talking freely. Choose a space where people can gather in a circle rather than sitting in rows.

Choose a day and time. The day and time make all the difference in who is included in the group. Daytime groups tend to include stay-at-home parents, though some who work may attend over a lunch hour. People who work and single parents often cannot attend during the day. Sunday morning groups often get couples and single parents due to children receiving care in Sunday school while parents attend their own class. Weeknight groups that offer childcare accommodate parents who work as well as single parents. When scheduling weeknight meetings, plan to end early enough for parents to get children to bed on school nights. Choose a day and time that balances the schedules of parents who want to participate with the availability of the discussion leader. Allow a minimum of 60 minutes, and preferably 90 minutes, for meetings.

Choose frequency. Groups that meet weekly or bi-weekly tend to get more closely bonded and connected than groups that meet monthly. Also, parents with children with higher levels of needs benefit from more frequent access to support. The special needs community is very fluid with health and behavior issues often keeping a parent away from groups at the last minute. If a group is only meeting monthly, various circumstances may limit a parent to only participating a few times a year.

Make a childcare decision. As with choosing a day and time to meet, whether or not your group will offer childcare impacts who can participate. If a congregation is not equipped to offer childcare, a daytime or weeknight group may be the best options. Children are in school during the day and couples can "tag team" on weeknights so that one parent can attend. Churches can still include single parents by offering to assist with the cost of hiring a sitter.

Create a plan. There are a variety of ways to organize a group. Book discussions keep the group focused on common material and learning new skills for coping, which helps meet emotional and spiritual needs. Guest speakers help meet informational needs on topics of common interest to special needs families, such as estate planning, guardianship, navigating social security disability, advocating for educational needs. A group can also be as simple as opening with a devotion and then inviting parents to share about their week. Groups work especially well when they rotate among these, reading a book for several weeks, then inviting in a guest speaker followed by a few less structured meetings before beginning another book. I wrote *Special Needs Parenting: From Coping to Thriving* specifically to help churches launch support groups.

Invite, invite, invite! Create awareness about the group by adding it to the church website, promoting through social media, bulletins, and announcements. Reach outside the congregation with a press release to local newspapers, flyers in coffee shops, therapist's offices, and local schools. The best way to grow a group is through personal invitation.

Get social. Encourage parents to connect outside of group meetings by setting up closed groups on social media. With parent permission, share the group roster of email addresses and phone numbers among members. Schedule a social gathering such as dinner or movie night several times throughout the year.

Be seasonal. Groups often have a rhythm to them. Parents are more available at the start of the school year and after the holidays. Support groups that are crowded in September and October are often empty in December and over the summer. Plan for off time so that discussion leaders get a break. It can get discouraging to plan a meeting and have low turnout. Use these off times for a monthly social night out to help the group stay connected.

Through leading support groups for many years I've seen time and again the healing that happens in community.

Though parents within the same group often have children with a variety of diagnoses, the emotional and spiritual journey is similar. That journey is made all the richer by sharing the path and encouraging each other.

Dr. Lorna Bradley is author of *Special Needs Parenting: From Coping to Thriving,* an ordained deacon in the United Methodist Church, wife, and special-needs parent. Despite generally feeling slightly behind on writing deadlines, she greatly enjoys running, travel, scuba, and watching amusing cat videos. @revdoclorna, facebook.com/LornaBradleyAuthor, SpecialNeedsParenting.me

CHAPTER 25

THE ROLE OF A FAMILY MINISTRY PASTOR

A BIG PICTURE PERSPECTIVE

BY **NINA SCHMIDGALL**

RECENTLY, AT AN EVENT AT OUR CHURCH, I lost sight of my son. I had been moving quickly and thought all my kids were trailing behind me, but, turning around, I realized I was missing one. After a few minutes of looking, I spotted him. He was up in the balcony, leaning precariously over the edge looking for me. He caught my eye and grinned. It had worked! He'd found me! Why had he gone up there? Because he had gotten separated from me and hadn't been able to see through everything happening around him. He knew that the higher view would give him a better look, a big picture perspective.

Perspective is important. There is value to having someone in place who sees the big picture. It's the reason there are offensive coordinators and defensive coordinators, special teams coaches, but still one head coach who is responsible for the big picture and is calling the different plays. It's the reason that, even with a team of incredible teachers, a school will have a principal that coordinates the teaching goals for each grade. It is the reason that, even though they are the ones paying the bills every week, couples look to a financial planner to help them address their long-term spending and savings goals.

There is value in having someone in place to drive key players toward the same end goal. It is important to have someone committed to keeping a team aligned and heading in the same direction.

It is for this reason that many churches are shifting their approach to serving families and children. In older models of ministry, the pastors or leaders of the various age groups tended to focus in on the needs of their distinct age group. There was a youth pastor and a children's pastor and maybe even a family counseling pastor. They all had their own goals, plans, and calendars. This would result in the leadership pulling in different directions, implementing different strategies, using different language, and moving toward separate ends. It was easy for parents to feel confused or even stressed by competing visions and events. Kids were lost in transitions between age groups as they grew.

More recently, churches have been asking great questions about how to develop a comprehensive approach to minister to families for the long haul. What if we had a plan to partner with parents through each phase of a child's growth and development? What might it look like to care for a family from birth through graduation with one comprehensive strategy?

At the church where I serve, we host an event where we share with new parents the different ways we want to partner with them as their child grows. As a part of the evening, we describe our commitment to partnering with their family as their child navigates the transition between age groups. We paint a picture of the milestones, moments, and challenges through which we want to support them. This is one of my favorite ministry moments, because even the most hesitant or skeptical parents sit up in their seat and lean in, their attention captured by the realization that we really have a plan to support them as their child grows all the way into adulthood.

As an increasing number of churches realize the importance of identifying an individual committed to developing a discipleship strategy from cradle to graduation, there are many questions about what that role might encompass.

IMPORTANCE OF SPECIALISTS

This is not to diminish the importance of age group leaders and pastors. There is a very important role for specialists to be experts of their age group. They know the specifics about what young people that particular age need, the challenges they are overcoming, the things they value most. But while age-group committed pastors and leaders are the experts for the kids in their age group, it is the family ministry pastor who shares the big picture with parents. Parents walk with their child through each unique season. They have hopes and desires that go beyond the time their child will spend in preschool, elementary, or youth group. They are concerned with the development of their child at every season and every phase. A family ministry pastor is in the best position to keep the parents at the center of the conversation.

So, what is the role of the NextGen or Family Ministry Pastor?

GUARDIAN OF THE MINISTRY CULTURE

The NextGen or Family Ministry Pastor is committed to being the *champion of the Next Generation.* One of the most valuable parts of a leader coordinating all the age groups is that someone is committed to serve as protector of the culture of your family ministry. They are the guardian of your ministry DNA. He/she will define and protect an overarching purpose and strategy so that all age groups are working toward a common goal. He/she will prevent you from silo tendencies where each age group is only working toward their own priorities. That person will protect and advocate for the needs of families in large church decision-making moments.

PROTECTOR OF ALIGNMENT

The NextGen or Family Ministry Pastor will *fight for strategic alignment*. Competing interests within the family ministry at your church puts stress on parents and can create confusion. The efforts seem random and the calendar becomes crowded. A NextGen Pastor inspires staff and volunteers to avoid age-group silos by leading the team to work together for the same purpose and end result. They need to be collectively responsible for the same objective. They will value the importance of having key players in the same room on a regular basis to cast vision, set goals, develop strategy, and wrestle with roadblocks and hurdles.

So, how do you know if your family ministry is aligned? Here are some indicators to determine whether your ministry is strategically aligned at this point.

- Does everyone on the family ministry team sit around the same table regularly?
- Do the calendars and budgets complement or do they compete?
- Is there a clear, designated leader?
- Have you clarified the win for parents at each stage?
- Do you have an easy and clear transition between age groups?

LEADER OF LEADERS

The NextGen or Family Ministry Pastor must be able to **lead a team of leaders**. Just because an individual is gifted at working with kids does not necessarily mean they have what it takes to lead as a NextGen Pastor. A NextGen Pastor must lead up to champion family ministry to senior leadership and cast vision down to all members of the team. They need to have a heart for leadership development and also the skills to supervise and manage people.

RESPONSIBLE FOR A PRO-FAMILY CULTURE

The Family Ministry Pastor is really a minister to the whole family. They are responsible to **create a pro-family culture**. At National Community Church, where I serve as Family Ministry Director, we do not host any event that is not focused, at its core, on partnering with parents. It is my top priority to think of them during the decision-making process, to advocate for them, and to innovate new ways to support them.

COMMITTED TO TRANSITIONS

One of the most important reasons to have a pastor leading with a cradle to graduation perspective is to ensure a big picture commitment to transitions. It is during transitions between age groups that churches have the greatest risk for kids to slip out the back door of the ministry. It is also the greatest opportunity to capture and engage new families in a new way. A family ministry pastor will champion the entry, transition, and exit strategies for a family ministry.

FOCUSED ON PARENTS

While age-group committed pastors and leaders are the experts for the kids in their age group, it is the family ministry pastor who shares the big picture with parents. A family ministry pastor is the best advocate to keep the parents at the center of the conversation.

If you have a NextGen or family ministry pastor who is new to the role or you are hoping to move in that direction, here are some steps you can take to make your NextGen pastor successful.

Ensure the NextGen pastor has a seat at the table of church decision-makers. A Family Ministry Pastor cannot properly advocate on behalf of families or create a strategy to make families a priority at your church unless they are invited into the decision-making process.

Ensure the Family Ministry Pastor is equipped and enabled to manage teams. They should be capable and empowered. Management and strategy skill should be an important part of hiring. Senior leadership must communicate the importance of the role, grant authority in decision-making, and give substantial room to lead. A family ministry pastor should have the freedom to hire and fire and to build their team so they might align toward a big picture vision.

Encourage the Family Ministry Pastor to make shared language a priority. Articulating the culture and DNA of the ministry requires a common language across age-group ministries. It is shared language that will align age groups toward a common end and bring teams into understanding of shared priorities. It also offers parents much needed clarity.

Give the Family Ministry Pastor the support to meet regularly with their team leaders. At first, age group leaders might be resistant to gather together with other pastors and leaders. But it is only by being in the same room regularly that a team can come together around a common vision and overcome challenges with the wisdom that comes from a wide lens.

Big picture leadership requires wisdom that comes from a wide lens—a balcony-level perspective. When families see that your church is committed to their child at every phase and stage and have a strategic plan to maximize their investment, they will feel confident to partner with you!

Nina Schmidgall serves as Director of Family Ministry at National Community Church in Washington DC. She has overseen the family ministry department since 2001, growing it to 8 locations. Nina and her husband, Joel, live on Capitol Hill with their 3 kids: Eloise, Ezekiel, and Lorenza. When allowed time off for good behavior, Nina enjoys dance, cooking, and bargain shopping.

CHAPTER 26

RETHINK YOUR STAFFING STRATEGY

BY **KENNY CONLEY**

THE WAY WE STAFF KIDMIN IS ALL WRONG!

At least that's what I thought about five years ago when I came across some new insights in relation to a staffing dilemma I was facing. I was leading the largest staff I'd ever had, but I felt like we weren't winning in the way we should. Sometimes, it can be the result of having the wrong people on the proverbial staffing bus, or it could simply be that we're using an outdated structure that is inefficient. This realization has prompted me to begin taking an entirely new look at the way I hire. No, I haven't uncovered a secret formula, but I have uncovered a few principles that have served my church very well.

This is how I knew that the traditional model is broken. Imagine with me as I paint the scenario we see happen at churches all over the country.

Veronica gets hired as the first ever children's pastor. She's been doing it as a volunteer for years,　but now she's finally on staff and getting paid for it. The church is growing and at this point, Veronica is primarily leading in elementary and she has some strong volunteers holding down the fort in preschool. The church gets a little bigger, the budget grows, and Veronica hires a part-time preschool director to oversee everything that happens with kids before elementary. The church continues to grow over the next few years and Veronica eventually hires an elementary director and even an assistant, so she can focus on leading the entire ministry.

What I just described is how most kidmin departments grow. Very few deviate. There's nothing really wrong with this model, but it isn't as efficient as it can be.

I have bigger concerns with what happens next, where I believe the traditional model begins to break down. The church grows and money becomes available to hire additional positions. Sometimes, new roles are added that benefit the entire ministry, like a volunteer coordinator or a childcare coordinator. However, growing ministries will often begin hiring staff under the elementary and early childhood directors, forming larger departments. This is where children's ministries can become highly inefficient.

Five years ago I read the book *Lead the Way God Made You* by Larry Shallenberger which prompted my new quest for creative staffing solutions. The premise is that most of us are really good at a few things and not so good at everything else. Unfortunately, we probably only spend 20% of our time doing the stuff we're really good at. What if we staffed in such a way that most of the staff spent 50%, or even 80%, of their time doing the stuff they really loved and the stuff they were really good at? Further conversations with other staff leaders helped me see things I hadn't yet noticed. I found that almost all ministry roles land in one of three ministry buckets.

BUCKET 1: ADMINISTRATION

Systems, organization and procedures that work in the background allowing ministry to actually happen in a safe and efficient way

BUCKET 2: PRODUCTION

Creativity, fun and compelling environments where truth is communicated to kids in ways that stick

BUCKET 3: VOLUNTEER RELATIONS

An army of willing men, women, and teenagers who make ministry happen every week and must be recruited, trained, organized, and cared for

People generally have a bent toward one of these buckets, yet we rarely have roles that allow staff to primarily operate in one of these ways. The traditional elementary director frequently teaches from the stage on the weekends, constantly recruits and trains volunteers, while keeping everything organized. More often than not, the preschool director is doing the same exact thing. What if we moved away from the roles of elementary and preschool directors and thought about roles that allowed staff to operate mostly in one of their gifts? It was an interesting premise that challenged my thinking.

As I began thinking creatively about staffing, it led me to develop questions to ask myself when hiring and evaluating staff positions. Here are three key questions I began asking every time I was ready to hire a new team member.

I. IS EVERYONE ON MY STAFF DOING WHAT THEY DO BEST?

This is a tricky question as you might be biased if you have good relationships with your staff. It's also tricky because your staff might not answer it the way they should either. It's natural for a person to fear losing a title, even if it means they'll spend more time doing what they enjoy. Let's be honest with ourselves though. Someone who is absolutely amazing at administration, production, and volunteer aspects of ministry is like a leprechaun or unicorn. They're legendary and likely don't exist. You might get really lucky and find someone who does two of the three really well, but more than likely your people probably only play best in one of these three areas.

If this is true, let's play this out. Veronica's elementary director is really talented when it comes to production and her preschool director is amazing with volunteers (highly characteristic of these positions, I might add). Because of the staffing model, this ministry will have really great productions in elementary with subpar productions in preschool. Additionally, they will have an excellent volunteer culture in preschool but a struggling volunteer team in elementary. To top it all off, both directors will feel disorganized due to administrative challenges. As great as the directors are, they'll never feel like they're winning. They'll feel like they're drowning and it doesn't have to be that way.

What would happen if the elementary director walked away from his title and took full ownership of productions for all of children's ministry? What if he could spend most of his time developing volunteer teams to lead incredible productions in multiple environments? What would happen if the preschool director walked away from her role and took full ownership of all kidmin volunteers? What if she developed the recruiting, training and care processes for every age group and environment? Yes, the transition would be challenging and details would need to be worked out to ensure that people and tasks didn't fall through the cracks. However, it's likely that the entire ministry would benefit from better production experiences. It's also likely that a healthier volunteer culture would exist everywhere instead of in just one department. Oh, and your staff would probably enjoy their jobs more because they get to spend more time doing what they love. My favorite part of this organizational idea is the kind of community that develops between the staff. They have to depend on each other to be successful, and they'll feel more like a team working together instead of two people overseeing different departments. Win, win, win!

2. DO AGE GROUPS REALLY MATTER?

Early on when the organization is small, we might answer this question with a "yes." You'd want to hire a preschool director who excels with all the munchkins and you'd want the elementary director to be highly relevant to that hard to please 5th grade boy.

However, if you have a long-term view of your organization, you might answer the question with a "no." Hopefully, you're building an organization where the volunteers are building relationships with the kids. The characteristic you're looking for most in a director is their ability to lead volunteers, not their relevance to a specific age group.

A good volunteer director can recruit and develop volunteer coaches/leaders, who will lead volunteers, who will build relationships with the kids. This volunteer director can put the right coaches and volunteers in elementary and the right coaches and volunteers in preschool. Age groups don't matter as much as we think.

The same is true when it comes to productions. Whether you're putting together a production for elementary or preschool, you need tech, hosts, storytellers, worship leaders, and actors. A good production director can easily produce programs for any age group.

3. AM I THINKING OUTSIDE THE BOX?

Maybe you only have a part-time position available to fill a role and you're finding it really difficult to find someone part-time. Maybe you've got the perfect candidate for a full-time role, but he's only available on a part-time basis.

I think we should get more creative with our roles. Is there someone else on your church staff who is in a similar part-time role? What if you coordinated with them to take on your open role making them full-time? Maybe the full-time position you have available could be divided into two or more roles to adequately support what needs to be done in a creative way. Don't limit yourself to predefined roles that are less efficient than you can afford.

FINAL THOUGHTS ON STAFFING

I want to help Veronica and others like her. It's a very peculiar problem with a very specific solution. She has enough staff to have a children's ministry that knocks it out of the park every week, but because staff are in positions where they aren't utilized to their full potential, they'll always struggle.

Since I began asking these questions about staff, everything has changed. I'll never go back to the traditional model. I have staff who have responsibilities that span multiple age groups. I have staff who spend almost all of their time doing what they do best. I have a production director who spends half her time working with artists and volunteers in our adult arts department and half of her time leading productions in kidmin. Because she spans both areas, we have access to volunteers and talent that wouldn't gravitate to the children's ministry. I love that some of the people who sing on our main stage also sing on our elementary stage.

Turning the traditional and accepted staffing model upside down is one of the best things we've ever done. Begin to think differently about how you staff your ministry. Get the most out of your staff, design roles where they love what they do, and create a staff environment where people have to work as a team to be successful. It could be the adjustment your ministry needs that changes everything.

A kidmin leader for nearly two decades, Kenny Conley currently leads all NextGen ministry at Mission Community Church in Gilbert, AZ. Outside of his many ministry pursuits, Kenny enjoys taking adventures with his family through travel, hiking, and just about anything outdoors.
childrensministryonline.com, @kennyconley

CHAPTER 27

COACHING THE WEAK-SIDE FOOT

BY **RON HUNTER JR.**

THE WHOLE WORLD WATCHED AS U.S. Women's team member Carli Lloyd scored three goals within just 16 minutes to defeat Japan in the 2015 FIFA Women's World Cup. This particular game would also be the last World Cup match for Abby Wambach who holds the record for most international scores with 184 goals. Wambach entered the game with just 10 minutes left in play. Lloyd voluntarily removed her captain's armband to place it on Wambach's arm, and cheers erupted. The transfer showed honor, care, and self-lessness.

Cheers should also explode from the crowds when parents pass their faith along to their sons and daughters. What does family ministry look like and what can be done to build great players in the world of family ministry?

The church is "the stadium" where players assemble weekly, but just like in soccer or any other sport, unless practice and disciplines are developed apart from game time, the odds of a win are rather slim. What is the fundamental skill all aspiring soccer players must learn in order to become a competitor at the college or national level? The use of the "weak-side foot." Watch Messi, Ronaldo, Beckham, Chastain, Wambach, or Lloyd as they dribble the soccer ball down the field at full speed. You'll have a hard time discerning which is their dominant foot, because they've worked on passing, kicking, and dribbling with their weak-side foot to the point that it can no longer carry that title.

CHURCH—THE STRONG-SIDE FOOT

The dominant foot in discipleship—the church—might be reliable, but how much more could be done if the discipleship responsibility was shared? What can the church do to increase family ministry effectiveness? The first task is to change the culture of relying on the church to do everything. This shift starts with ministry leaders, and if possible from the pulpit. Each ministry leader can have a meeting with all those soccer moms (and dads) to build them up; tell them you want to help them, and then follow through with coaching.

At church, make sure you teach beyond just knowledge and comprehension. It is not enough for children today to just learn the stories of the Bible or memorize scripture; they need to know how scripture affects their actions, feelings, and attitudes. Teach parents to discuss the lessons at mealtimes and to carry the key theme through the week. Use a curriculum that makes this easy by teaching the same biblical themes to all ages (D6 2nd GEN, Gospel Project, Orange, Tru, and others all do this). When a parent is learning the same concept as their child in an age-appropriate way, they gain confidence and are more willing to discuss scripture with their kids. This is especially true for new Christ-following parents. Spend time with parents showing them how to use the curriculum tools and helps for the home. Do not assume they understand. They're often scared to attempt this. Role-play between parent and ministry leader is an excellent coaching tool.

Find key benchmarks in a child's life and help the parents take the lead in walking their child through this time—benchmarks that include tying one's shoe, riding a bike, starting kindergarten, middle school on up to driving, and graduation. These milestones are launching pads for relationship connections by parents (and grandparents). Be available to help them navigate the experiences with their child. Meet with parents about how to prepare for these events. There are tremendous benchmark type resources from ParentMinistry.net, Milestones, and Faith Path that can help with this task through rites of passage.

Don't try to replace the parent by holding all life-shaping events at church. Teach parents and grandparents how to shape their kids' lives. The number one spiritual influence in a child's life (for good or bad) is Mom and then Dad. Challenge the parents to get on board and help you teach and connect. They are your ministry multipliers.

HOME—THE WEAK-SIDE FOOT

Okay, you coach the parents at church. Just like a sports coach, you give them drills or items to do at home. What are some practical tips parents should know beyond the obvious win of a curriculum that works both at home and church? If the only time a child has a conversation with their parent is when they are in trouble or being "preached" to, the child will dread those moments. So teach parents to connect both for fun and teachable moments. Remind the parents that not every conversation has to be a sermon.

Most ministry leaders are either extroverts or adapted introverts who have learned to connect well in conversations. The Myers-Briggs personality assessment reveals that 51% of participants are introverts. Forbes suggests a similar study where they estimate one-third to one-half of the population are introverts. That means about half your parents do not know how to easily connect in conversations even with their own kids. Imagine the relationship development that could occur if you helped parents over this hurdle.

Explain the value of playtime, solving puzzles, reading together, and other opportunities to share space, words, and feelings. Try to have them shoot for together moments that allow conversations. Encourage parents to plan time for these connect moments, or they will always be too busy. Show the parents how to ask about their child's "highs" and "lows" from their day, then give them permission to dig deeper into the answers. If their child felt disappointed, angry, excited, or scared, parents can coach them how to respond in action and attitude beyond the initial emotional upheaval.

Challenge parents to read Scripture daily and share a verse with their child at least twice a week. The sharing should be about what the parent learned and not what the parent wants the child to learn. Our children need to see us interacting and listening to our heavenly Father and how that discipline helps us make life decisions; otherwise, where will they learn to make such decisions?

PRACTICE AND DISCIPLINE

I coached soccer for 11 years, and I would say to my teams every season, "The difference between a good soccer player and a great soccer player is the use of your weak side foot." After every practice, I asked the players to go home and kick the soccer ball at their trashcan placed about 15 yards from them. They were not to stop until they hit it 10 times in a row. That was easy for the dominant foot: three minutes and they were done.

But I also asked them to repeat this drill with their weakside foot which often took 20+ minutes. Getting the parents to do their part at home takes a lot more energy than simply preparing your lesson for church (that's your dominant side).

Ask yourself if you can do less ministry by helping parents do more—at home and church. Ask your lead pastor to join you in the cause. This could be accomplished by providing a "lean in" time for parents and grandparents during the sermon or a handout in the program providing talking points for the home centered around the sermon or from their life group.

Regularly meet with parents of the children you teach, either one-on-one or in groups. Help them understand how to use any take-home piece that you send, whether paper or digital form. Let them practice in a group of parents or with you on how to use it. Teach them to ask open-ended, fun questions with their kids, and then how to listen and ask follow-up questions.

So let's rephrase: The difference between a good church and a great church is the use of parents, your ministry multipliers.

COACH EVERYONE TO BE GENERATIONAL GLADIATORS

Many soccer players optimistic of playing at the collegiate level or beyond fall short because of their weak side foot. While the church retains more teens moving up to the next level than the soccer world, we can still do better. Just as in every sport, there are some who will take all your inspiration and coaching advice and give it their all both at church and home. Others will show up and work hard only at church. We still coach everyone like potential champions. Parents and kids alike will emerge as generational gladiators when the home becomes as much of an emphasis as the church.

Ron has authored or helped author 3 books: *The DNA of D6: Building Blocks of Generational Discipleship, Youth Ministry in the 21st Century—5 Views,* and *Toy Box Leadership.* Ron Hunter Jr. is the CEO of Randall House (publisher of D6 2nd Generational Curriculum), and he's the Director of the D6 Conference. However, his favorite titles are husband and father. D6Family.com

CHAPTER 28

7 HOLIDAY "GIVING" TIPS

SUPPORT KIDS WITH SPECIAL NEEDS AND THEIR FAMILIES

BY **MARIE KUCK**

HOLIDAYS CAN BE A STRESSFUL TIME of the year, but for families that have kids with special needs it can sometimes be less than a "merry" holiday season. Not only may these families experience a strain on the already diminishing pocketbook, but the stimulation that the holidays bring can be overwhelming to kids. Added caregiving demands needed for these kiddos may not allow parents adequate time to prepare for the holiday, leading to unmet expectations for a happy family time.

This can be the perfect time to teach kids about the real gift of giving. Here's a few quick ways to engage your kids and families in some meaningful ministry moments with kids who have special needs and their families.

1. Give the "gift of time." Provide a night of respite and offer childcare for kids so that parents can have time to get their holiday preparations and shopping done. During this time, assist the children in creating a special gift for their parents, such as a photo and frame.

2. Give the" gift of service." Offer to do practical errands. When you're running out for that Black Friday special, ask if there is something you can pick up as you shop.

3. Engage in the "gift of giving" by adopting a child with special needs and their family. Consider choosing to give gifts to a family rather than exchange gifts within your family. Kids can be part of picking out special presents, wrapping, and delivering.

4. Offer the "gift of hospitality." Provide some homebaked goodies to a family that might not have time to prepare these holiday treats. It can be a great "hands-on" family activity that kids of all ages can get involved in. Be sure you inquire about food allergies.

5. Share the "gift of your presence." Put together a Caroling Caravan and bring Christmas cheer to a family that might be in isolation. Consider caroling at someone's doorstep or visiting a local children's hospital.

6. Give a "secret gift." Bless a family by anonymously providing some necessary food provisions or gift cards that might help with some of the financial challenges of the season.

7. Give the "gift of experiencing Jesus." Think ahead of ways to make provisions to welcome kids with special needs and their families for holiday services and programs. Secure some extra "buddies" to assist visitors. Find ways to include these kiddos in holiday programs and pageants. Don't forget that inclusion means participation.

Marie Kuck is a mom on a mission. She's the co-founder of Nathaniel's Hope, a growing national ministry that cheers on and assists kids with special needs and their families and helps churches get equipped to do the same. She anticipates being reunited with her son Nathaniel, who moved to heaven at the age of 4 1/2. Nathanielshope.org

CHAPTER 29

FAMILY MINISTRY

BY **AIMEE LEVINE**

ALTHOUGH WHAT NEEDS TO BE done may sound simple, it's not always easy to carry out. However, the rewards are great. We believe in doing life together and yes, that does mean things get messy sometimes. But we're a family, in Christ, and family dynamics do get messy sometimes. Here's my list of what goes under the simple-but-not-always-easy-to-do" lessons that I've learned the past year.

PRAY!

I'm sure anyone looking at me over the past year has seen what appears to be me talking to myself. Trust me, I was praying ... praying for the ministry, the church, the volunteers, the program, the curriculum, the children and their families, myself to be able to serve joyfully and in the direction that He wishes us to go, our church leadership, etc. The list was long! Starting and ending with prayer and praise realigned my thoughts to where He wanted the ministry to be, not what I wanted.

This led to making the addition of praying as a large group with all the teachers, assistants, and children in the same room. Instead of just praying in our small groups according to age, we all prayed together. Because all of the teachers and volunteers got to hear the prayers of all the children, not just those in their own class, they started to get to know each other better. Slowly, relationships started to build as a children's ministry team, not just classes for children.

IT'S ALL ABOUT THE RELATIONSHIP!

Building relationships is an investment ... one well worth dedicating a large portion of time. Relationships cannot be forced, hurried, or superficial. Children are extremely perceptive. They know when you're not being true and they also know when you really care.

One switch we made was that we utilized the time between when the children are dropped off for class and the time when we start our kids' church program. Previously, this time was taken up by showing a video before we got started.

Yes, this time is more chaotic! No, the children aren't sitting quietly awaiting class to start. Why? Because we're all talking and sharing what has gone on during the week. We use a large beach ball with questions written all over it. We toss the ball and have the child, teacher, or assistant read a question off the ball. Then we take turns answering. You learn some pretty interesting things if you ask the right question!

Apparently, most of the children and adults have actually tried dry dog food and prefer it over canned, if push came to shove. Our poor worship director happened to be in the room at the time of that particular question. The look on his face was priceless and I did actually see a smile.

We also involve anyone who pops their head into the class. No one is safe and the kids really enjoy that! We bring the parents in and anyone stopping by into our games.

The time that we share before the program actually begins is priceless. The key is to use this time to get to know one another. There is no perfect activity or perfect way to play. As long as we are sharing, it's all good. That leads me to ...

PERFECTION IS SUCH A SCARY WORD.

God is perfect. Jesus is perfect. We are not. Letting people see your mistakes and how you handle them is part of doing life together. This is something our church really focuses on. The children need to be in on it, too. Just because we're their teachers doesn't mean we know everything. Working on the lesson together and sharing ideas is where real learning takes place ... not the perfectly planned lesson, with the perfect craft and perfect snack.

Perfection is a good way to burn out, not only yourself but your volunteers as well. This isn't to say that there shouldn't be a standard for volunteers and a plan for the lesson. However, there should be room to adjust to where the Holy Spirit's leading the class.

CARING MEANS SHARING.

Honestly caring about the children and their families and what's going on in their lives is vitally important. Listening to parents share what's going on in their lives and letting them know the things going on in yours, is important. I love the fact that we're working together and that the children's ministry team is not only made up of teachers, teacher assistants, and registration people, but the children and their families as well.

In a growing church, it's so important to be able to praise God with someone when something is going well and also to pray with that family when things are hard. It's challenging to stay and socialize after church or get involved in a small group setting if you have young children. There may be options available for these young families to get to know others in the church but more often than not, they're only seeing the people in children's ministry. I feel very strongly that we need to get to know these families. That means that we need to take the first step in building that relationship.

HAVE FUN!

Wait ... what? Fun in children's ministry? Say it isn't so! Well, yes it is so.

Our children's ministry team is comprised of teachers, teacher's assistants, registration team, worship team (small, but large in talent), parents, and children. With that being said, the fun is not only for the children. Parents and children need to see that we actually enjoy what we're doing.

I remember an exercise that we did over the course of a month. We were to find out from various ministry leaders throughout the church and several staff members what the perceptions are regarding volunteering in children's ministry. I knew I was having fun along with the teachers and children. But I was afraid to ask what people actually thought about what was going on over there, "in that hall!"

When that assignment came up, we had already switched to a very interactive curriculum, had worked really hard on building relationships, and let parents know repeatedly that we were there to come alongside their family.

The response was so great. Being over in the children's ministry hall and volunteering was fun. Lots of exciting things were going on over there. Whew! That was so great to hear, but even better than that, there was excitement and energy building. There is really only one way to build that level of excitement and energy, and that brings up my next point.

SHOW YOUR PASSION!

Your passion comes through in everything you do. It needs to be there. If it isn't there, please find it before you go on. Trust me, there are days when we all may not be on top of our game. We may not be as prepared for the lesson as we want to be. All of that needs to take a back seat compared to our love for God, the children, and their families. If that shines through, the rest is secondary.

LOOK AT THINGS FROM A BIRD'S EYE VIEW.

I remember one of the very first changes that we made (after adding prayer to our large group), was to take a good look, using all of our senses, at our children's ministry classrooms and hall. We looked at the flow of traffic to make things easier for parents to drop off and pick up. We looked at safety for the children. And we looked at the classrooms.

We did eventually add a new check-in system which helped with safety and the flow of traffic for parents dropping off and picking up children. However, the biggest thing we did was to change the classrooms to "moveable" classrooms. We made benches that were durable and lightweight so the children could move them by themselves and that we could easily change the set-up of the classroom depending on what we were doing for that day or activity.

I hadn't realized the huge impact that this would make. Because the benches were lower, made of wood, and not overwhelming in size (compared to the adult-sized tables we had before) plus a few other factors, the children were more relaxed and teachers were teaching at their eye level, not stooping over them while they were working. The results were immediate. Currently, we're considering building some more benches as we grow!

IF YOU BUILD IT, THEY WILL COME.

I remember standing in front of the congregation saying that we were in desperate need of teachers. I still shake my head as I remember saying, in the nicest way possible, that if we weren't able to get the teachers that we needed, we wouldn't be able to offer Sunday School for elementary aged children. It was a desperate plea. I am still saddened by that day.

Over the next few months I realized that as our team prayed, built relationships, let people see who we really were (warts and all), sharing our lives, having fun together, letting our passion shine through, and changing things so they were a better fit for our families and community, those volunteers we so desperately sought after would come to us wanting to be part of what was going on. They would realize their unique spiritual gift would be welcome. I'm happy to say this is exactly what happened.

Even though these points are simple, they're not easy to follow through day in and day out. My prayer is that you will take them and use them for His glory, course correct when needed, and be joyful.

I'm Aimee Levine and I've been given a wonderful opportunity to use my 37 years of experience in working with people, plus the gifts God has blessed me with, to work with a wonderful church here in Northern Virginia. I wake up excited every day because I get to share my passion for creating unique ways to communicate His Word. This is more than a job; it's an adventure to share that passion by creating a place where families can grow together!

CHAPTER 30

TEACH THEOLOGY TO CHILDREN

3 STEPS TO TEACH YOUR CHILDREN SOUND THEOLOGY

BY **MARTY MACHOWSKI**

WHEN I SHARE THE IMPORTANCE of teaching our children theology, most parents give me a puzzled look, like I'm suggesting they teach neurophysics to a 3-year-old. When folks think theology, too often they picture dusty books written with small print and ten syllable words. While seminary shelves are full of those thick theology books, theology doesn't need to be complicated or difficult to understand. Take the word "theology" itself. It simply means "the study of God." So teaching your children theology is teaching your children the truth about who God is and how we can relate to Him. I've never met a Christian parent yet who didn't want to teach their children about God. They're just not sure where to begin.

The truth is, our kids are exposed to theology every day, and our culture is all too happy to dish out a diet of bad theology. For instance, our kids are regularly exposed to a worldview that assumes the universe created itself. They are told that mankind is basically good, and education is the answer to the world's problems. They learn that the earth is what is in need of saving and animals are more important than people. Television and movies regularly expose our kids to characters who live quite comfortably without God.

Before you panic, our kids are exposed to good theology too. Every time they look up into the night sky, it shouts, "God created me." That's how Psalm 19 opens when it says, "The heavens are telling of the glory of God; and their expanse is declaring the work of His hands." Kids can observe that people can do things animals will never be able to do, like have a conversation, read a book, write a poem, create a painting, and best of all, we can love. We alone are made in the image of God. Every time you as a parent pray for help, confess your sin, speak a scripture, sacrifice for others, or love your kids, you're teaching them good theology. You just need to help them recognize it.

I know what you're saying: "I want to help my kids learn good theology, but I don't know where to start." Theology is given to us in the Bible through a story. And like a good story, you first need to get to know the characters. Then you learn the basic plot and story line. After that, you can study the impact of the story on people and the claim the story has upon our lives. Follow that same simple pattern when teaching kids theology. Teach the youngest children the main characters first, teach growing children the story line, and train the older children to study and apply the message of Scripture to their lives.

HELP KIDS LEARN THE CHARACTERS OF THE STORY.
(2- TO 6-YEAR-OLDS)

Understanding the main characters of the story helps us understand what the Bible is about. This is how God's Word opens: *"In the beginning God created the heavens and the earth"* (Genesis 1:1, NASB). God is the main character of His own story. Teaching our children about God is the most important theological truth we will ever teach them. Even toddlers can start learning about the God who made them.

We learn a lot about God from the first chapters of the Bible. Genesis tells us that God existed before the creation and through Him all things were created (Genesis 1:1). That means we owe our lives to God, and we need to live for Him. As a painting reveals something about the artist, so the creation tells us something about God. God is amazing! He created the stars above (Genesis 1:14), the birds in the sky (Genesis 1:20), and animals that run on the ground below (Genesis 1:24-25). God formed the oceans and filled them with fish (Genesis 1:20). He created the moon for the night, the sun for the day (Genesis 1:16), and all of it was good (Genesis 1:25).

The first chapter of the Bible even gives us a hint that our One God is made up of three distinct persons. The opening chapter of Genesis mentions the Spirit of God (Genesis 1:2), and teaches there were multiple persons at work in the creation. Did you ever notice the plural grammar of verse 26 when God declares, *"Let us make man in Our image."* Later in the New Testament the Apostle Paul makes the Son's role in creation crystal clear when he writes, *"by Him all things were created"* (Colossians 1:16).

Simple Truth: The greatest scientist can't even count the stars, but God knows them each by name.

The second main character of the Bible story is mankind—people. It is important to teach our youngest children the truth we learn in the Bible about people. God created people.

That means that unlike God, we have a beginning. God made men and women in His image (Genesis 1:26), which means you can recognize things about God by looking at the people He created. As I described earlier, we can do things that the animals God created cannot do. Best of all, we can know and love God—and that's what we were made to do!

> **Simple Truth:** Parrots can only repeat what they hear, but the youngest of children can write a new song, never sung in the history of the world.

The third main character of the story is Satan, who in the form of a serpent tempted Adam and his wife, Eve, (the first couple) to turn away from God (Genesis 3:1). That's where sin entered the world and destroyed man's relationship with God and with his wife, Eve. Sin ruins everything. Because God is perfect and holy, He had to punish sin. So God sent Adam and Eve out of the garden, where without the tree of life they would die (Genesis 3:22-24).

> **Simple Truth:** Telling the truth has always been good, and lies have always been wrong.

TEACH KIDS THE BASIC PLOT AND STORY LINE. (5- TO 10-YEAR-OLDS)

Once your children learn the characters of the story, you want to teach them the basic plot line of the Bible. While the Bible is made up of 66 separate books, they altogether tell one story—the outworking of God's promise to save man from sin.

God's promise of salvation first comes to Adam and Eve right alongside His judgment of their rebellion in the garden. God promises that one of Eve's children will crush the head of the serpent (Genesis 3:15) and covers Adam and Eve's shame with animal skins (Genesis 3:21). God's covering of Adam and Eve with animal skins is meant to teach us that there is no forgiveness without the shedding of blood (Hebrews 9:22). From that time, every lamb sacrificed in the Old Testament in worship points forward to Jesus, the Lamb of God, who takes away the sins of the world (John 1:29).

Simple Truth: Jesus is the promised son of Adam whom God sent to crush the head of the serpent.

Similarly, every priest who offers those sacrifices points forward to Jesus, the great high priest (Hebrews 4:14). Every king who fails in Israel, points forward to the need for a king to come and lead his people to salvation. Jesus is the King of Kings and Lord of Lords (Revelation 19:16) who fulfills that need. Every prophet points forward to Jesus, who is the Word become flesh (John 1:14). The prophets knew that God was going to send a Savior for mankind (1 Peter 1:10-12) and foretold the coming of this Prophet, Priest, and King.

Simple Truth: The Bible is the story of how Jesus came to save us from our sin.

PRESENT THE CLAIM THE STORY HAS UPON THEIR LIVES. (8-YEAR-OLDS TO ADULT)

Once our children understand the main characters and the plot of the story, it's time to help them understand the claim the story has upon their lives. It is not enough to know good theology; we must respond by faith. Faith requires two ingredients. First, we must believe (John 3:16). We must believe that Jesus is the Son of God who took on flesh and lived a perfect, sinless life (Hebrews 4:15). Jesus died upon the cross to take the penalty we deserved (Romans 4:25), and He rose again on the third day, proving His victory over sin and death (1 Corinthians 15:4). But it is not sufficient to simply believe the facts of the Gospel story, we must also repent, or turn away from our sin (Acts 20:21). That's the second required ingredient of saving faith. The New Testament presents these two ingredients, repenting and believing, side by side from the moment John the Baptist introduced the ministry of Christ (Mark 1:15).

Simple Truth: You never have to teach a child how to sin; we are born with sin. That's why even children need Jesus.

So, we introduce our children to the main characters, teach them the Gospel storyline of the Bible, and challenge them to place their trust in Jesus. Then, through prayer we invite our all-powerful God to take that simple Gospel message, which is the power of God for their salvation, and soften their hearts of stone (Romans 1:16).

Marty Machowski is a Family Life Pastor at Covenant Fellowship Church in Glen Mills, PA, where he has served on the pastoral staff for over 25 years. He is the author of *The Ology* a systematic theology book for children and the *Gospel Story for Kids* series of books and curriculum. He is the father of 6 children. He and his wife, Lois, reside in West Chester, PA. martymachowski.com, theologyforkids.org

CHAPTER 31

DISRESPECT AND DISCIPLINE IN THE CHURCH ENVIRONMENT

BY **HOLLY ROE**

OW DO YOU CAPTURE THE HEARTS of children who are hard to deal with? Disrespect and discipline in a church setting can be difficult. If you're a director or leader in ministry with children or youth, you are no stranger to kids who are difficult to deal with. Many parents are struggling with not only how to be the spiritual leaders for their children, but also how to raise respectful children. As we strive to be influencers of the next generation and help raise up followers of Christ, there's no doubt that every person in ministry to children or youth will deal with tough kids at some point. Because ministry leaders typically only get these kids for a very short time span each week, we want to pour as much Jesus into their young hearts as possible while we have them. It's hard to do that if we're constantly trying to discipline as we teach. If you have children who are constantly controlling the entire learning environment and disrupting, here are a few techniques you can implement right away. You can begin to create a better learning environment and build the right relationships in order to influence the next generation in a profound way for the Kingdom of God.

Every family situation is different and we know that kids behave differently due to many factors. Some kids may have dedicated parents who attend church with them each week but do not have the parenting skills to know how to raise respectful kids. These kids are often allowed to run their household, therefore think they can run the show in any other environment they're in. They are easily recognizable because they're typically the ones who come in each week and lack self control. They will sometimes blurt things out at inappropriate times and act up so they can get the whole class going. Sometimes they have what I call "helicopter" parents who hover and rescue anytime they feel their child is not being treated superior to others. These parents sometimes complain about the ministry not meeting the needs of their child or say things like, "My kids just don't get anything out of it," or "They're bored." Lots of times these kids are not engaging with what's going on in the classroom and because they aren't as aware of what is happening, they do have a tendency to be bored, or at least think they are anyway.

You also may have what I call "drop-off kids" who have very little parental involvement and are just seeking attention and hoping someone will notice them. These kids want someone to take the time to make them feel special. Often these are the kids who leaders dread to see coming because they need the most investment.

There are many different family situations and personalities that we are privileged to work with as church leaders. It is often out of the complicated life stories of the most difficult children that we find the greatest potential for powerful testimonies of transformation. Some would say that these transformations usually happen as these children become adults and sometimes this is true, but we don't have to wait until they become adults for change to take root. As we invest in children and parents at the same time, this transformation can take place now in the lives of the families we minister to! The key is to partner with parents to make spiritual impacts at home with their children while they are young. They can empower their kids to be little ministers by providing opportunities for them to all serve and learn together. One of my pet peeves as a children's ministry director is when someone asks a child, "What are you going to be when you grow up?" The question we should be asking our children is, "What are you going to do for God right now?" Many tough kids just need to be uplifted, empowered, and made to feel special and loved. When we do that, they will rise to the occasion and begin to see themselves as a positive influencer of others.

When a child's negative behavior takes over the entire atmosphere of the classroom there are several questions we have to ask. First, are we engaging them in a way that they feel we're doing more than completing a job when we're with them? Second, are we keeping our cool during discipline and sharing our control, allowing strong-willed kids opportunities to lead now while they are young? Or are we treating them as if they have nothing to contribute to the Kingdom of God right now? Finally, are we investing time and building a relationship with them so that we can be powerful influencers in their lives?

In order to engage children in a way that lets them know that your time with them means more to you than just checking it off the list and saying that you did it, we must verbally let them know that we are passionate about teaching them biblical truths that will stick with them throughout their entire lives. Engaging children means that you put forth full effort every single time you meet with them and constantly seek out new fresh ideas. If you're unprepared, immediately they will notice and they are like intuitive sophisticated little radars. They will jump on the opportunity to "take you down." If you walk into that classroom prepared with a clear plan, engaging activities, and more than enough material to last the class time, you are a lot less likely to experience negative behavior.

Be prepared to use your radar as well and if an activity is becoming too disruptive, quickly move to the next thing. Good leaders can sense when it's time to move on. Using a variety of elements when teaching is key to keeping kids engaged. Science experiments, videos, small group activities, and sometimes pulling out a crazy looking puppet or throwing on a crazy hat and lip-syncing a silly camp song will capture them and bring them back to focus. Be ready for anything. The only way that this is possible is to be prepared. Creativity is a component. If you're simply talking for 45 minutes to an hour, I'd probably be bored and act out too!

For those times when you do need to set boundaries and discipline in your setting there are a few things not to do. One of them is lose your cool. When you raise your voice and threaten it can actually fuel misbehavior and cause kids to "up their game." Not displaying anger and frustration at their behavior is going to surprise the kids, because they're used to getting a negative reaction. Instead of lecturing and showing frustration, we can tell kids what we're going to do and they can't argue with that. This is called using enforceable statements. In discipline, we never tell kids what to do. Instead, tell them what you are going to do because they can't argue with that. For example, if you say to a child, "Pick up these toys," they can say a million things back to you in response. They could say things like "no", "I don't want to", "Not right now" "I'm too busy", "I didn't make that mess." If you say, "I'm going to clean this room in 15 minutes. I'll be keeping the toys that I pick up and you can keep the toys you pick up." They can't argue with that. In a classroom setting if you say, "I'm going to begin our fun game as soon as all of you are listening" and you follow through, it's more effective than yelling or telling them to be quiet over and over again. When we make threats like, "I'm going to tell all of your parents how terribly you've behaved today" and we don't follow through, we're teaching the kids that we don't mean what we say. If we do follow through and tell their parents, then it gives the kids someone to blame for their bad behavior. They'll say, "Well the reason is because he's boring and we don't have any fun in there." If this happens, you better watch out for the helicopters, because they'll be landing in your office to complain soon! When we make enforceable statements that you can follow through with, we teach the kids that we mean what we say.

Sharing our control is another great technique to avoid misbehavior, especially for those really strong-willed kids! They love control and power. Once I had an 8-year-old boy who acted out every week. He was a little aggressive toward the other kids and was always acting up. I engaged him pretty well using science experiments since we liked to blow things up and set things on fire, but he still had a little trouble. I realized that this kid needed a job. I built up this "job" really big. I told him I needed someone super talented and really dedicated to do this job. I told him that God's Word was the most important thing we talked about during our kids' church time and I needed someone really special for this job. It had to be someone who was strong and I told him I thought he was perfect for the job.

The first thing he said was, "Me? You want me?" You see, no one had ever thought he was perfect for anything. The only thing he heard all day long was "Stop," "No," "Don't," "Leave her alone," "Your parents are going to be so disappointed in you." For once, someone thought he was perfect. I told him the job was to hold up the Bible while I taught the lesson and turn to the right place and read when I told him to. He was thrilled. He said, "No one ever picks me to do stuff like that." He ran to his parents and told them all about his new job and the next

Sunday he arrived early and was super excited that he was important. It was the first week we had no interruptions during the lesson. He continued to be our Bible holder that year. Sometimes a kid needs a job!

Another way to share control is to give little choices. Strong-willed kids LOVE choices. For example, "Do you all want to leave the playground now or do you need another fifteen minutes?" Even though you were leaving in 15 minutes anyway, they don't know that, so let them feel like they have a little control over the matter. You might say, "Would you all like to read the Bible story straight out of the Bible today or do you want to act it out as I read it?" If they feel they have a little say-so, they're more likely to engage and feel that you think they are capable and valued enough to have input. I let them choose which worship song we will do the next week and sometimes I encourage them to come prepared to share what kind thing they did for someone else the week before. Let them know that they can do things now and don't have to wait until they're adults to do God's work.

The last and most important thing we can do to avoid misbehavior is to build relationships. This starts by simply noticing kids and what they're about. You may start off by saying things like, "I noticed you got new shoes" or "I noticed you like soccer. Tell me about that." Taking the time to notice things can be the first step in building a relationship. Most of a child's appropriate behavior is ignored and kids who are seeking attention don't usually care what kind of attention it is—negative or positive. They just want any kind of attention. These kids will do whatever will get noticed. When we make threats and reprimands, we're actually rewarding those children and giving them the attention they're seeking. If you make a point to notice things about them that make them special, you'll begin to build that relationship.

There's one thing that all kids, and adults for that matter, want—to be favored. As we teach them that they are highly favored by their heavenly Father, we must first let them know that they are highly favored by us! Every child should feel like they are your favorite. Lots of high-fives, calling them by name, and building them up in front of their parents and others can transform your relationship very quickly. It could sound something like this in front of the child and parents when they come to pick them up. "Andrew was so awesome today during our worship time. I loved seeing him raise his hands and praise God. You do realize that he has really special gifts and that other kids watch him and follow his lead. I'm so excited to have such a strong leader in our ministry. Andrew, God has BIG plans for you buddy." Then whisper, "You're one of my favorites!" I did this one time with a tough kid and it was the last time he ever misbehaved in my presence. He began to realize that I loved him. He went from putting stickers on my back when I wasn't looking to giving me big hugs every time I saw him. The parents also switched from defense mode to partnership mode. When they realize you really love their children, they are more likely to partner with you.

Kids will always live up to your opinion of them. If they know you dread seeing them coming, they'll live up to that expectation you have of them. If they know you think they are amazing, they'll strive to live up to that as well. People who know that others think highly of them don't want to disappoint those who see them in a favorable way.

In order to influence the next generation we must build relationships and spend time with those we are ministering to. Think of the people in your life who have influenced you the most. It's the people who have invested time to build relationship and gain your favor and respect that are most likely to have the biggest influence. Capturing the hearts of children begins with engaging them, empowering them, building our influence through time and relationship. If you can get a child to really love you and be convinced that you really do love them, discipline becomes less of an issue. After these things are in place, it usually just takes a soft whisper and light touch on the shoulder to a kid saying, "Hey, buddy, can you stop that for me, please? Thank you." to accomplish what yelling, harping, and threatening can't. To capture the hearts of children who might be hard to minister to at first, use the Jesus model. Stop, notice them, spend time with them, and love them unconditionally.

Holly has been in church leadership for over 18 years as a children and family ministry director, speaker, consultant, and coach. She is the Executive Director of JC Evangelistic Ministries and is involved with an equipping ministry called Forge that is changing the lives of young people all over the world. Holly is the wife to a full-time evangelist named Jason and the mother to 3 children.

CHAPTER 32

GENERATION TECHNOLOGY

BY **MATT MCKEE**

ELP! KIDS KNOW TECHNOLOGY BETTER than I do."
This is the statement I hear over and over and over. It's
no wonder, because times have changed and parents feel
overwhelmed when it comes to technology. Here are two sce-
narios to help you understand some of the differences, even if
kids have not changed all that much.

The year is 1985 and a 10-year-old boy asks his mom if he
can go outside and play. The mom says, "Sure, just make sure
you are home by dark." The boy heads out the door, and goes to
pick up a couple of friends from the neighborhood. They have
a ball, a stick, and enough curiosity to kill more than one cat.
They start to explore around the neighborhood and find a "secret hideout." They could tell they were not the first to find this
secret hideout because of words that were written on the walls
that they were not allowed to say. But the boys felt old enough
to handle it and hung out there for a little while until they got

bored. They saw another group of guys from the neighborhood and decided to put the ball and stick to good use. Not everyone was good at playing ball and they all didn't get along when there was a disagreement about a call, but they laughed with each other, told stories that weren't exactly true, and made it home by dark. The boy gets home and says, "Mom, I'm home."

The year is 2015 and a 10-year-old boy asks his Mom if he can get online and play with his friends. The mom says, "Sure, but I would rather you guys not play those teen-rated games." The boy agrees, pulls out his mobile device and heads to the TV that has the gaming console attached to it. The boy video calls his buddies to make sure they are all online. They all have a mobile device, an Internet connection, and enough curiosity to kill several cats. They start exploring the online world and find some "secret hideouts." Not only do they find words left behind from those who had been there before, but also pictures, videos, and links to other secret worlds. There is enough to explore in this online world that they could get lost for days, weeks, and maybe a lifetime. On their journey together they run into other kids from other countries who happen to be online at the same time. They all explore together, laugh together, build together, and fight together. The mom walks in the room and tells her son that it's time to log off and eat dinner.

In the first scenario the mom had her worries, but she knew the neighborhood. She also knew that her son couldn't go too far. She had talked to him about not taking candy from strangers, not getting into fights with the other boys, and staying away from the house of the one guy who no one really knew. The curiosity of the boy and his friends could only take them so far before boredom or the urge to do something else kicked in. There was plenty of trouble that the kids could have gotten into, but there were also other adults in the neighborhood who were looking out for them.

The second scenario is very similar to the first. The mom still has her worries, but she really doesn't feel equipped to know where her son is truly going. She doesn't really understand all the dangers that are out there. Her son has the same amount of curiosity and the same need for community. The difference is that his curiosity will only grow the more he explores. There is plenty of trouble for the boy to get into and there are very few adults working together to protect him.

We all feel parenting is different today, but many of us can't really explain the difference from when we grew up. It would be easy to blame the technology for all of the differences today. However, technology can be used in amazing ways, and innovation is not going to stop. The advancements we have today are incredible tools that reflect who we are as a society. Sometimes, we love the reflection that we see and other times it reminds us how broken our world is around us.

How do we help parents and kids in this ever-connected world that we live in? If only there was a device, a simple conversation, and a group of adults watching out for each other and their children. Wait, maybe that's the answer.

TECHNOLOGY HELP

Today there are plenty of technologies that will filter the Internet for kids. Most devices even come with parental controls, so as long as parents have a degree in technology, they'll be able to stay ahead of their kids. There is good news for the rest of us, though. Let me introduce you to a parent's best friend: Circle. Circle is an internet-connected device controlled by an app that helps parents do the following:

Time Limits — Put time limits on apps, games, and websites.

Insights — See how your kids spend time online.

Pause — Pause the Internet with a single tap.

Bedtime — Choose a bedtime for your kids' devices.

Filter — Set individual filter levels by age per device.

All Devices — Manage all the devices in your home.

These are all powerful tools in a parent's hands. Knowing where your kids have gone, what type of information your child is engaging with, and setting limits on the amount of time children spend online can make a huge difference in a family. Circle solves a lot of the technology issues for parents, but a device can't solve all the problems.

CONVERSATION

Just like in 1985, parents still need to be able to talk to their kids. Parents need to feel equipped and empowered to have conversations with their child about where they've been, who they've been with, and what they've experienced.

Here are 3 questions that could help start the conversation between parents and their kids.

- What is the most interesting thing that you've seen recently?
- Who said something that surprised you recently?
- What is the coolest or craziest thing your friends are doing now?

Notice that none of these 3 questions ask specifically about technology. Kids today don't divide their experiences into online and offline memories. They think in ways that are connected in both realms. You will get answers about both. Again, this isn't about technology. It's about having a relationship with your child so you can step in when they get into trouble, either online or offline.

COMMUNITY

We have a great device, a conversation, and now if we had a group of adults helping each other. I believe we have a community that has now been equipped to help each other parent. Jeff Shinabarger, the founder and CEO of a non-profit in

Atlanta, says, "We will be known by the problems we solve." Since the church believes it has the greatest message of all time and the hope for all people, then we can solve this problem. It's ironic when ministry leaders say that technology is the enemy, because the church has been the leader of innovation in many areas over the last 2000 years. It's only in recent history that the church has taken a back seat in innovation and lost its relevance. I believe the church has an opportunity to lead by partnering with parents to help keep their kids safe, both online and off.

Let me encourage you as a children's pastor or parent. The good news is that you are not alone and you have the chance to connect with others who want to solve this problem. In all reality, no parent can protect their kids on their own. That problem is not new. Parents, to truly make a difference for our kids we have to model the actions that we want to see from them. Pastors, that means that we must model the actions that we want parents to have as well. As 1 Corinthians 10:13 (NASB) says, *"No temptation has overtaken you but such as is common to man; and God is faithful, who will not allow you to be tempted beyond what you are able, but with the temptation will provide the way of escape also, that you may be able to endure it."* We still have the hope of the future and a God who is pursuing each and every one of His children. God knows we need His help and I think it's now time we ask Him for it.

Adam Duckworth and I recently started a movement called ParentChat. It's a way to bring about encouragement, education, and a little fun to parents who feel lost when it comes to technology. We travel around the country doing parenting events, talking about things like Circle, how to have a non-threatening conversation with your kids, and how parents can help each other. We believe it really takes all three approaches if we're going to make a difference. If you want to partner with us in helping keep kids safe online, visit ParentChat.tv to learn more about how you can help parents, kids, and your community with online safety. If you want to learn more about Circle and all of the benefits that it can bring to your family, visit meetcircle.com.

 Matt McKee is a writer, speaker, entrepreneur, and just another guy who is trying to make a difference. His latest book is *Parent Chat: The Technology Talk for Every Family.* He has a pastor's heart, a business mind, and entrepreneur hustle. twitter.com/mattmckee, facebook.com/mckeelive, mattmckee.me

CHAPTER 33

IO+ TIPS FOR HOLDING THE CREATIVE MEETINGS OF YOUR DREAMS

BY **COLLETTE TAYLOR**

THE FIRST TIME I WAS invited to a "Creative Meeting," I had no idea what to expect. It sounded like fun; who doesn't like to create? But I quickly realized "creative" and "meeting" can have lots of different meanings. Luckily, my first exposure to creative meetings was for a program called "KidStuf" at North Point Community Church.

I figured out right away that a creative meeting is only as good as the facilitator of the meeting, and my first meeting had a great facilitator. Reggie Joiner was that facilitator and the same person who had envisioned the event from the beginning. Reggie navigated a lot of ideas (some great, some terrible), from some very diverse personalities. He somehow made people feel like their terrible ideas weren't all that bad and would get us to an end result we all liked. (I think some of those terrible ideas were mine. I remember hearing quite often, "There are no bad ideas.") You could freely share your ideas without feeling inadequate or insecure. There were many times we might talk about a dozen less-than-great ideas, but each one got us one step further to the best idea yet.

Since that time, I've been a part of hundreds of creative meetings organized to produce events, design family ministry environments, plan staff retreats and build camps from the ground up.

I've been in some excellent creative meetings, and then there were ones where you hoped someone would accidentally set off the fire alarm so the building would have to be evacuated and the meeting would end. Hopefully, these suggestions will help you successfully facilitate a creative meeting to come up with the best possible ideas without needing to set off the fire alarm.

THE CREATIVE TEAM

One of the first misconceptions of putting together a creative meeting is that you need a lot of people to come up with a lot of ideas. But it's actually easy to have too many people in the meeting. There are a couple of reasons for this.

- Too many people cause distractions.
- Too many side conversations take place.
- People talk over each other.
- You have to provide more snacks.

HOW MANY PARTICIPANTS ARE TOO MANY?

While there's probably not a definitive answer to this, a good number to start with is six to eight. You may have to schedule a few meetings and try it out with different numbers of attendees to find a balance. One of the things we discovered is that it's best to ask people to attend one or two creative meetings (even though long term, you may have 12 scheduled for an event or project). That way if you realize that it's too many, you don't have to un-invite them.

HOW DO YOU KNOW WHOM TO INVITE?

Not every person on your staff needs to participate. As a matter of fact, there are some people on your team who would rather run across hot coals than to be part of a creative meeting. They are usually your more concrete thinkers. They don't really love to brainstorm. They will spend the entire time in the meeting thinking of the to-do list on their desk that isn't getting done. Then there are those who are more "realistic." They are hard workers, but would rather work on the budget than think about how to get a camel in the room for the Christmas story.

You want participants who aren't concerned with coming up with the best idea themselves, but understand that it's a process. Their ideas may not be used as originally stated but it helped to get to the best idea that will now be put into play.

Many times, you'll need to look outside of your organization for people to invite. Remember the KidStuf creative meetings I mentioned earlier? When I was first invited to those meetings, I was not a staff member. I was a mom who had two kids the age KidStuf was geared toward. We also had two other moms, a stage host, an actor, and a worship leader. We were all extremely varied in our personalities and our talents. What we each brought to the table meshed well together to create a family experience.

So, you've scheduled your first few creative meetings for an upcoming event. You've invited the people you think would be the best ones to have around the table. Now what?

THE CREATIVE SPACE

Select a meeting space that is warm and inviting. A space with windows is always good for creative meetings. You want it to be relaxing and fun. You may be thinking, "Well, none of our spaces are super fun and exciting." That's okay. You can make it fun by bringing small toys for people to play with. Or cover the plain white table with craft paper and throw crayons in the center. The key is to let people in the meeting loosen up and feel free to share ideas.

To set up the space for our meetings, we use storyboards and multicolored index cards. You can also use a white board.

THE CREATIVE MEETING

Define the Meeting

One of the most important things you can do at the beginning of a creative meeting is to define the kind of creative meeting it is. If you fail to do this it could be a frustrating experience for those facilitating and whoever is participating. Here are a couple of examples.

Blue Sky Meetings

When planning for an environment, special event, or Sunday service, you'll need several different kinds of creative meetings. In a "Blue Sky" meeting, any idea is welcome. This is not the time to talk about budget or time limitations ... just broad ideas.

Decision-Making Meetings

The next set of meetings is where you'll narrow your options. In these more decisive meetings, you'll eliminate ideas that aren't possible due to location, facility limitations, budget, or other reasons.

Action Meetings

The decisions have been made, so it's time to put hands and feet to the ideas. At this point, you can schedule follow-up meetings to check on everyone's progress.

Knowing the type of meeting makes a big difference. You don't need action steps at a Blue Sky meeting, and you don't need new off-the-wall ideas at an Action meeting.

Guard the Focus

"Wait! I thought we were supposed to be creative! Focus?" Yes, because believe it or not, focus can fuel creativity. That's why you need to start with a white card on the board that clearly defines the goal of what you are trying to create or the problem that needs to be solved. Without that direction, you can waste a lot of creative energy. Some people have the idea that the creative meeting is supposed to be free-flowing where anything goes. Creativity without focus can lead to confusion. The best meetings have just enough order so that even ideas you don't use are worth keeping. You'll still chase some rabbits in creative meetings, but focus means you chase the kind of rabbits that lead you down a path and uncover a hole that will lead you back. Effective facilitators have to guard the focus without shutting down the flow of ideas.

Capture the Ideas

It's also important to have two notetakers: one person who takes detailed notes and another person who can write the ideas on index cards (or whiteboard) and post them up as they are being thrown out so none of them get lost. You will be surprised at how much you can miss if no one is taking detailed notes. It's also pretty entertaining to go back and read the notes later. You'll find yourself wondering how on earth you thought you were going to be able to fly someone into the ceiling to demonstrate Jesus' ascension into heaven.

Debrief Next Steps

Once your event is over, the final type of meeting is a Debrief. This is where you'll celebrate the wins and then discuss what could have been better, especially if this is an on-going event or environment. Keep debrief meetings positive. How can you be positive when talking about things that went wrong or things to improve? You do it by not placing blame and not beating something to death. In these meetings, we encourage people to bring solutions if they bring up something that didn't go quite right. You want the people in the meeting to leave encouraged, not discouraged. While every little thing may not have gone right, in the end, you probably had an incredible event that changed the life of a child.

The brainstorming, creative process can be a bit overwhelming in the beginning. But remember: the God who CREATED everything, including you, has called you to create environments for kids that will bring them closer to Him. I can't think of a better reason to find a way to dream up the very best ideas.

Colette Taylor is the Executive Production Director for Orange, which means she produces the Orange Conference, Camp KidJam, and Orange Tour. Basically, she produces things. And she LOVES football. ThinkOrange.com

CHAPTER 34

4 WAYS TO REST

HELP! I'VE BEEN IN KIDS' MINISTRY FOR YEARS AND NEVER TOOK A SABBATH!

BY **LORI ANN PISCIONERI**

W E'VE ALL BEEN THERE. We serve our faces off, day in and day out and it seems to never end. We tell ourselves, "If I can just make it to Easter, I'll take a break then." We believe that no one else cares about kids' ministry as much as me, and it must get done, no matter what. While it is absolutely true that ministry is a 24/7 job, we must be obedient and honor God with rest.

Deuteronomy 5:12-14 (NASB) lays is out for us. *"Observe the Sabbath day to keep it holy, as the Lord your God commanded you. Six days you shall labor and do all your work, but the seventh day is a sabbath to the Lord your God."*

If rest is not a priority, then we undervalue the call that God has placed on our lives and we let the enemy work his way in. Not only have I watched this happen to several ministry friends, it happened to me.

Last year was the hardest year of my life. I started 2015 in a seemingly great place. Our kids' team was thriving. Our focus on teaching kids about Jesus, mentoring them, and partnering with single parents was going really well. I even had an opportunity to perform in an opera (my full-time pursuit before God called me to kids' ministry). So I took it. And I got hurt. Physically. I was performing in a role that required a lot of dancing and I injured a tissue in my hip that got progressively worse throughout the year ... because I never truly found rest. During the three months of rehearsals and performances, I continued to lead in kids' ministry. After all, I am the children's pastor (see my cape blowing in the breeze), so what could my team do without me?

Physically, I could no longer stay at the pace I was used to. Despite all the prayers, pleading, crying out to God for healing, and anointing of oil, I faced surgery and was being forced to take six weeks off. Completely. Not by choice, but by necessity. If only I would have had the foresight of building margin in my schedule and prioritizing rest on a regular basis! Intellectually, I understood the concept of *"I can do all things through Him who strengthens me"* (Philippians 4:13, NASB) but spiritually I missed the boat.

In the months leading up to the surgery, I leaned on God BIG TIME. I sought after Him like never before and asked Him to show me how to navigate this situation with peace. How was I to step away and be healed through my surgery and recovery when I had two new staff members and a team that I wasn't sure could manage without me? How could I be absent from the hurting children, the lost and broken families entrusted to my care, especially at such a time of transition at our church?

As I asked God and listened for His voice, I received the answers. He constantly reminded me of His love and faithfulness.

I had to learn to truly rely on Him. He is merciful and gracious, and He placed me in this role, in this church, in this city. I had to rest in Him. Ecclesiastes 3 was a constant comfort to me: *"For everything there is a season, and a time for every matter under heaven ... a time to heal ..."* It was not easy, but I finally surrendered and found rest in the Lord.

If you are in a state of constant worry, stress, busy-ness, never allowing yourself to truly rest, then perhaps what I learned during this time will be helpful.

Here are 4 ways to find REST.

1. CULTIVATE A RELATIONSHIP WITH GOD.

We all know that we can't have a lasting relationship in any shape or form if we don't give it daily attention. If I only spend one day with my spouse, my marriage will suffer. Marriage takes daily attention and loving commitment. In building a relationship with God, it's the same—daily attention and loving commitment. God loves us and is constantly pursuing us with His love. He expects the same from us.

I didn't realize that it is on THIS foundation, my relationship with God, where I can truly find rest in Him. God could instruct me in how to rest. I found that there is no separation and that it is through relationship that I can grow in my ministry and still set boundaries and times of rest for myself.

John 15:5 (NASB) says, *"I am the vine, you are the branches; he who abides in Me and I in him, he bears much fruit, for apart from Me you can do nothing."* The fruit we all need is there for us when we don't separate ourselves from our relationship from God.

2. EAT WELL, PHYSICALLY AND SPIRITUALLY.

Spiritual food and physical food seem to be in contrast to one another, but actually, when we eat well, spiritually and physically, we are nourished in body, mind, and spirit. 3 John 1:2

(NASB) reminds us, *"Beloved, I pray that in all respects you may prosper and be in good health, just as your soul prospers."*

When I heard the Holy Spirit's call to serve in kids' ministry, I felt that I needed to clean up my diet, spiritually, and also in what physical foods I was eating. Junk food, even TV shows and an overload of social media that take my focus off God's call on my life, are not good for me and certainly don't bring me rest.

My spiritual diet is best when I spend personal time with God everyday, reading His Word, and allowing space to hear from Him.

When I eat well, I rest well, which includes sleeping well too! Bonus! My mind is not cluttered, stressed, or distracted. I'm not hyped up on sugar or too much caffeine. I am balanced and fed. Kids' ministry runs best when the leaders are at their best physically and spiritually. Eating well and resting well are crucial.

3. HAVE A SPIRIT-LED STRUCTURE.

God has gifted me in the areas of systems and structure and I have relied on that to build a team of hundreds of volunteers that minister to 400 kids and families each week. My mind thinks in spreadsheets and charts. I understand that not everyone is gifted in that way and I have learned to speak the language of grace when many people in my realm of influence don't have a clue where I'm coming from. I have learned that because I am gifted in this way, I tend to discount how valuable it is to allow margin in our structure for the move of the Holy Spirit. Our team needs space to receive His guidance, to hear His voice, not mine as their leader. Kids need a response time to what they are learning, so they can encounter Jesus in a tangible way. God's presence is often missed when every moment of a service, meeting, and conversation is planned out and executed to a "T."

God showed me in the six weeks that I was in bed after my surgery that when I plan every waking moment of my day, I have no margin to hear from Him, let alone find rest. The idea of *"Come to me, all of you who are weary and carry heavy burdens, and I will give you rest"* (Mt. 11:28, NLT) was truly being lost on me, because I would come to Jesus, but not be obedient in what He was trying to give me—rest in Him!

In preparation for my absence, I began loosening the structure of the team a bit, to be more guided by the Holy Spirit and God showed up in a BIG way! Our leaders began to report more ministry moments than before. Our kids had revelations and were able to verbalize their faith more than ever before. Our kids' staff was able to thrive in their strengths and share with me how much more empowered and led by God they felt. Hearing these testimonies, I rested more and more in Christ and relied more on His strength than ever before.

4. TRUST YOUR TEAM.

Taking a step away from ministry, whether forced or not, helps gain perspective. If I had not had the six weeks off to rest and recover, I would not have seen the trust I have in our kids' team. I would still be plugging away in old habits, relying on my own strength to accomplish the work of the ministry. And I would be exhausted in my physical body in doing so.

In Matthew 7:7, Jesus instructs us: *"Ask and it will be given to you; seek and you will find; knock and the door will be opened to you. For everyone who asks receives, and to the one who seeks finds, and to the one who knocks, the door will be opened."*

During my time of rest, I prayed and diligently asked God to care for our kids' ministry, to build faith and trust in our kids' staff and team to carry on in my absence, to be stronger in love, more passionate in serving, and deeper in commitment in caring for our kids and families. I asked and

I received. It is through my rest that I found the answers to prayers and now have the opportunity to teach others to rest too.

Prioritize REST. Believe me, it's worth it!

Lori Ann Piscioneri is the Children's Pastor at Oasis Church in Los Angeles, CA. She is passionate about building God's Kingdom through kidmin, spending time with her amazing husband, and enjoying all that Southern California has to offer: film industry, music, great vegetarian food, and everything outdoors!

CHAPTER 35

UNDERSTANDING KIDS

BY **PAUL HARKNESS**

GOOD GRIEF! I DON'T THINK I could do that!" said the Awana leader as he stood before his small group of third grade boys looking into a clubber's book during Handbook Time. "Those are long verses. And there are two of them in this section."

Later, as he met with the Awana Commander, the leader stated, "I think we're asking way too much of the kids in my group. That's a lot of memorization work. And some of the concepts they are supposed to know are beyond these kids."

Overhearing the conversation, a young mom, who is an Awana leader of third grade girls, stepped in the room exclaiming, "What do you mean? We need to push some of these kids more. They are not stupid. They can do more and understand more than we give them credit for."

Two adults, working with the same aged children, with two quite different opinions about the capabilities of their third grade students. Are the kids being overwhelmed? Or are they under challenged? Who is right? How do you know what they are capable of?

Adults need to understand the children they are working with as they teach them truth. This understanding will alleviate frustration for some adults and encourage others to challenge kids at a higher level.

Understanding children involves many aspects, but let's begin the task by considering the characteristics of children. There are five characteristics of children that should be understood. Understanding children in the areas of the spiritual, mental, physical, social, and emotional will help us to better reach and teach them. These changing characteristics will help us see what we might expect in each stage along the way from preschool through the sixth grade. Keep in mind these characteristics are in general terms for each age group. Every child is his/her own individual, uniquely created in the image of God.

The following information comes from three helpful resources: one from Awana Clubs International leader training, a second from the book, *Wholly Kids—Guiding Kids to Life in Christ*, published by LifeWay Kids, and a third resource, personal observation of my own wonderful, near perfect grandkids.

PRE-SCHOOL (3-4 YEARS OF AGE)

Preschoolers are a fun little bunch of love and energy. Three- and four-year-olds are my wife's favorite group to work with each week.

Spiritually, they are beginning to understand that God, Jesus, the church, and the Bible are special. They enjoy handling and using the Bible. They like to hear and retell stories from the Bible. Preschoolers are recognizing that God and Jesus love and help people, so they too may see the need to help others. They enjoy Bible verse games and are beginning to sing songs about Jesus. And, very important to note, they are learning to trust in many ways at this point. They can learn to trust Jesus as their Savior.

Mentally, preschoolers are developing quickly. Most have a vocabulary of 1,000-2,000 words, although you might think it is much more if you're around your own 3- and 4-year-olds. They are beginning to explore their world which may lead to their own creativity. They are also developing a sense of fear and have bad dreams. Preschoolers cannot yet separate out fact and fantasy. They are able to memorize Bible verses and songs.

Physically, they are making big leaps—literally! They have the coordination to hop, skip, and jump. They use their large muscles and their fine motor skills are just beginning to develop. Attention span is increasing. These are all good things to keep in mind when choosing games for these little ones to play.

Socially, personal relationships begin to develop. They play rather well with others and want to please the adults around them. They also like to include imaginary companions in their circle of friends. Most of the time they can share and take turns.

Emotionally, preschoolers can be rather intense with their feelings. They can be very loving and the next moment they can have a meltdown. Like all ages of children, they like to have fun, so they laugh a lot. Preschoolers are gaining more self-control; however, when they get really frustrated or angry, will fall into a temper tantrum.

LOWER ELEMENTARY (KINDERGARTEN – SECOND GRADE)

This group has begun school and they are anxious to learn. There's a lot of energy here as well.

Spiritually, they can know God. They ask questions about God and like learning from the Bible. They are drawing conclusions about God and are beginning to make application of the Scriptures to their own young lives. Lower elementary children may begin to understand the relationship between God and Jesus, and might wonder why Jesus would have to die for others' wrongdoing. They can understand the Gospel. They understand that people become Christians by trusting in Christ and can be guided to a concern for others. In their continued desire to please adults, it can be easy for us to lead them to a false confession of faith. So we must be clear that it is a matter of trusting in what Christ did for us, not a matter of praying a prayer. This age group can worship the Lord. They enjoy singing songs in groups especially catchy melodies that they will sing at other times. They are remembering stories from the Bible and are beginning to sequence the stories. They may even begin to see the relationship between the Old and New Testaments.

Mentally, lower elementary children ask a lot of questions. They want the answers to all of those "why" and "how" questions. Careful ... they are literal-minded, but they have active imaginations. They like to discover, then, they like to explain things—you know, Show-and-Tell. They like to take things apart to see how they work. They like new games, games that are not only fun but challenging. Guessing games are fun for them and they like to tell corny jokes. Not all are readers but they are growing in that area.

Physically, they are controlling the large muscles better and are improving the fine motor skills. They have good eye-hand coordination. Distinguishing left from right begins here. They tend to get ill more often and experience more real and imagined injuries. These children are energetic, but tire easily. Again, these things should be kept in mind when selecting games for the children to play.

Socially, the kindergarten through second grade child is self-centered but having friends is important to them. They like to talk. Approval from an adult and encouragement is needed. They thrive on encouragement. They are very anxious to do well. This is when they begin to enjoy competition.

Emotionally, this group likes excitement. Everything can be so exciting! They are enthusiastic. Yet they are often unhappy, easily upset, complaining, and take any failure hard. They are sensitive to the feelings of others and will quickly sympathize with them. They look to their teachers for help and will often imitate them.

UPPER ELEMENTARY (THIRD – SIXTH GRADE)

There's a broad range of changing characteristics in this group. It might be wisest to divide the group in half. However, since this is an article and not a book I will attempt to summarize.

Spiritually, they want to know the truth. They may not know the word "justice" but they know what it means. They want things to be fair, in their eyes at least. "It isn't fair!" How many times have you heard that? They think in terms of right and wrong. They are developing a conscience and a value system. Continued guidance is needed. Upper elementary children are looking for direction and spiritual answers.

Mentally, their attention span is increasing. They think in abstract terms and discern the difference between fact and fiction. They are thinking deeper thoughts. They can accept criticism when worded carefully. They are creative, curious, and imaginative, and can express ideas, solve problems, and make plans. This group is developing in their reading and writing skills.

Physically, girls are growing quicker than boys. They are full of energy and anxious to display their physical skills as they become more coordinated. Again, all of this is important in selecting games.

Socially, they like competition. It is at this point in life they are making strong friendships. Heroes are important to them and they follow their heroes and know everything about them (idolize them). They are great talkers and need to be allowed to talk. They develop interest in community. They can accept rules and responsibilities. They like to win. Their attitudes toward the opposite sex are changing.

Emotionally, this age group can change moods quickly. They are easily influenced emotionally. They recognize and can begin to appreciate differences in individuals which may be why they also struggle with self-confidence.

We should equip ourselves to understand children so we may work with them effectively and patiently. Characteristics are just a part of that understanding. There are also socioeconomic factors, the reality of different types of learners (visual, auditory, etc.), and the simple differences between girls and boys.

Children are complex. God asks us to invest in them. Understanding them better will add joy to both the teacher/leader experience and the child experience.

 Paul Harkness and his wife, Janet, live in Ord, Nebraska and serve as missionaries with Awana Clubs International. Previously, they served in pastoral ministry for 20 years, and then conducted a variety of seminars in local churches. In addition to their Awana ministry, Paul teaches a course on personal evangelism in Germany every October for one week. They have 4 grown children and 7 grandchildren.

CHAPTER 36

KIDS' MINISTRY AND CHURCH VISION

BY SANDY HALL

A nd he said to all, 'If anyone would come after me, let him deny himself and take up his cross daily and follow me'" (Luke 9:23, ESV).

As the Kids' Ministry Director, I have the privilege of seeing first hand every Sunday the wonderment of children getting to know Jesus, either for the first time or learning more about Him and what He did for us all those many years ago. There is nothing sweeter to my ears than hearing a child at pick-up sharing the Bible story they learned with their parents and having them recite scripture to these grown-ups! So many times kids' ministry is an afterthought at most churches, just a place to keep the kids out of "big church." I am blessed to work at a church that recognizes the value of a strong and thriving kids' ministry. Our lead pastors know that having a strong kids' ministry assists in having parents come back to church because they feel their children are getting what they need spiritually and, in turn, they attend and also get to hear the Word.

One of the most important things a church can do is share their vision with its members and having that vision be a part of every ministry on campus. As Andy Stanley, senior Pastor of North Point Community Church, stated, "Vision is a clear mental picture of what could be, fueled by the conviction that it should be. Vision is a preferred future. A destination. Vision always stands in contrast to the world as it is. Vision demands change. It implies movement. But a vision requires someone to champion the cause." Vision is a conviction, a passion. Vision is discovering what God is already constructing. For over a year our church has shared the following vision across all ministries.

GO AND MAKE MATHETES.

"Mathetes" is the Greek word Jesus used to describe a group of His followers. The word "mathetes" is translated into English as disciple. This person is "all in" when it comes to following Jesus. Our job on this earth is to create mathetes and that doesn't start when a person is an adult; it starts with the children. There is absolutely no reason a child cannot become a mathetes. We expect our children to learn to play ball, learn an instrument, and exceed at school. Why would we not expect our children to become followers of Christ—mathetes? We're joining an ancient movement that started with Jesus.

"And Jesus came and said to them, 'All authority in heaven and on earth has been given to me. Go therefore and make MATHETES of all nations, baptizing them in the name of the Father and of the Son and of the Holy Spirit, teaching them to observe all that I have commanded you. And behold, I am with you always to the end of the age'" (Matthew 28:18-20, ESV).

WHAT ARE SOME OF THE QUALITIES OF A MATHETES?

1. A mathetes is Rescued.

We were dead and Jesus came and made us alive all by grace, not by works. This is such an awesome concept to teach in kids' ministry. We get to tell the kids how God sent His only Son down to earth and let Him take away our sins. There is nothing they need to "do" to get into heaven. They just have to believe in what God did and live out His promises for us. It's incredible how much easier a time children have in understanding this than adults do.

"But God, being rich in mercy, because of His great love with which He loved us, even when we were dead in our trespasses, made us alive together with Christ—by grace you have been saved" (Ephesians 2:4-5, ESV).

2. A mathetes is Awestruck.

Being awestruck means living a life of worship after you have been rescued. By teaching our kids that our God has rescued them, it causes them to become awestruck by what an incredible sacrifice He made for us. As John Piper, author and teacher of desiringgod.org, stated, "When we teach people to not only believe in our Lord, but also delight in our Lord, it creates a new passion for the pleasure of God's presence in their lives." Who better to reflect that sense of passion than children? Children who are passionate and awestruck about the Lord will share His story and help create more mathetes because their awe of who God is will be contagious!

3. A mathetes is Mobilized.

Our church's unofficial motto is that we are "Rescued to Rescue." We are now on a mission! Every one of us is on a mission and YES that includes our children in the kids' ministry. Being mobilized means we are ready to spread the Word of God and make mathetes, whether that is going on a missions trip or having our children be part of mission projects. For the past couple of years within kids' ministry we have held mission projects twice a year. Every one of them is a different project. It may be a local missions where we collect cereal boxes or sports equipment. Or it may be missions abroad where we make stuffed turtles for kids in Haiti or friendship bracelets for kids in Guatemala.

We are very intentional in making sure the kids are big contributors to whatever project we do and we try to tie the project into our curriculum during that month. Some may say that the kids aren't "really" the ones doing the mission project; after all, it's the parents who have to buy those cereal boxes or sporting equipment. Some part of that is true, but with the help of our volunteer teachers, we make it a point to explain to the kids what they are doing, why they are doing it, and for whom they are doing it. It's wonderful to hear the kids explaining to their parents the reason why they have to go to the store to get a cereal box or a basketball. We take pictures of everything so the kids can remember what they did and whom they served in the name of Jesus.

My favorite mission project by far has been a very simple one. Last spring, our Missions Ministry was heading to Guatemala. Our kids' ministry team saw this as a great opportunity to invite someone from the Missions Team to come and speak to the kids, show pictures, and explain to them what a typical day for a Guatemalan child is like. That Sunday, I saw kids who have everything under the sun just stop and take notice of children, just like them, who have absolutely nothing, yet those children were smiling, happy, and sharing God's love. I saw transformation that Sunday in our kids. They were super excited to make the Guatemalan kids some friendship bracelets and what was more inspiring was watching them help their fellow church mates in making the bracelets. Our missions team took the bracelets to the kids in Guatemala and were able to take pictures, and videotape the kids at the center making friendship bracelets for our kids here. It was so wonderful to show that to our kids and give them the bracelets the kids in Guatemala made for them. It wasn't a shiny new tech gadget. It wasn't the latest greatest toy. It was a simple threaded bracelet from a child from another country, but you would have thought our kids had just won the greatest prize ever! That experience taught us that our kids could be mobilized and also understand what that means.

I shared the vision of our church with you so that you recognize that your church's vision is also your kids' ministry vision and it can be incorporated in what you do. Don't ever let anyone use the excuse, "Well, they're just kids." YES! They are kids, but guess what? They get it! If you invest in them now, they will be the ones to lead others to become Mathetes, become Rescued, be Awestruck by God's love and Mobilize people to become Mathetes in their own right!

"And calling to him a child, he put him in the midst of them and said, 'Truly, I say to you, unless you turn and become like children, you will never enter the kingdom of heaven. Whoever humbles himself like this child is the greatest in the kingdom of Heaven'" (Matthew 18:2-4, ESV).

Sandy Hall is a lover of all things pink and sparkly. She's wife to Ed, mom to Amanda and Dylan (the best teenagers on the planet), and when she's not wearing her wife and mom hat, she's the Kids' Ministry Director at West Pines Community Church, Pembroke Pines, FL. With a Masters in Marriage and Family Therapy she knows the importance of making a difference in those God brings into her path each day.

CPSIA information can be obtained
at www.ICGtesting.com
Printed in the USA
BVOW11s2324220916
462888BV00002B/4/P